FINDING CHARITY

Joe Remesz

Order this book online at www.trafford.com
or email orders@trafford.com

Most Trafford titles are also available at major online book retailers.

Printed in the United States of America.

ISBN: 978-1-4269-0124-9 (sc)
ISBN: 978-1-4269-0126-3 (e)

Trafford rev. 02/23/2011

 www.trafford.com

North America & international
toll-free: 1 888 232 4444 (USA & Canada)
phone: 250 383 6864 ♦ fax: 812 355 4082

ABOUT THE AUTHOR

Joe Remesz was born in Bonnyville, Alberta in 1931. He graduated from Lorne Greene's Academy of Radio and Television Arts in Toronto and began his broadcasting career with the CBC in that city. Later Joe worked for radio stations in Niagara Falls and Fort William, Ontario, Yuba City, Calif, Stateline, Nevada and Trail, B. C. where he was a news director at CJAT for many years. In 1978 Joe retired from radio broadcasting and moved to Penticton, B. C. where he took up selling real estate as a career. He has traveled extensively throughout the world and presently fully retired resides in Edmonton and Canlupao, Southern Leyte, Philippines.

Three things Joe still would like to do are: Learn how to swim, watch a whooping crane egg hatch and take part in the Midnight Yellowknife, NWT golf tournament.
Until he reaches his goal Joe keeps writing novels and short stories. Four of his works: A Bucketful of Ogopogo and Goalie Stories, Karma's/Matt's Divorce, Tension Rising and Cul-de-sac are almost ready for publication.

FOREWARD

I have worked in the broadcasting and real estate industries and enjoyed both. I met a lot of people, had my ups and downs and in the end managed to laugh at myself and with others.

There are joke, anecdote and amusing story books about the broadcasting industry. I could write about my experiences as a radio/TV announcer but feel broadcasting has already been adequately covered by other writers but not the real estate industry.

In *Finding Charity* I hope you and your friends will enjoy reading with hours of smiles, chuckles and old fashioned belly laughs.

Whenever I appear as a guest on radio or TV talk-show the host often invites me to 'stay a little longer' as listeners and viewers jam the phone lines with material. It seems that each humorous incident happened in their town, to them or a friend.

Many theories exist about what humour is and what social function it serves. I found that people of all ages and cultures respond to humour. The majority of people are able to be amused, to laugh or to smile at something funny and thus they are considered to have "a sense of humour." Science proves that laughter heals. Sometime a sense of humour is a requisite for long-term survival in the real estate industry.

After you have read *Finding Charity* I do not take responsibility for a cardiac arrest.

I have tried to give credit wherever possible but jokes, anecdotes and amusing stories generally and now with cyberspace technology sweep the world so swiftly that it is often impossible to discover who put the story into public print first, let alone who actually originated it.

I had fun in planning *Finding Charity* and to all those whom I interrupted with "I already got that one", I apologize.

I'm particularly grateful to my wife Teofista for planting the idea in writing *Finding Charity*.

EDMONTON

Paris is great and so is New York. Edmonton, however, is larger in area than Chicago, Philadelphia or Detroit. Edmonton is my home so take my hand and I'll show you around. We belong to Alberta. By our highways there are wild roses, emerald lakes, winding rivers, mountains and green forests. Alberta is grand and so is Edmonton

Edmonton, Edmonton you are okay having celebrated one-hundred years as city of champions, marching, marching strong and free into another century.

As we walk the streets of Edmonton, the city I love, there are indoor and outdoor activities for all seasons. It's a city of festivals where one can watch the stars and a lunar eclipse at the Telus Science Centre or search our ethnic heritage at the Museum and the Archives. And if that isn't enough there's the Alberta Art Gallery and live performances at the Winspear Centre, home of the Edmonton Symphony, the Citadel Theatre and the Jubilee.

Edmonton, Edmonton you are okay, having celebrated one hundred years, as a city of champions, marching, marching strong and free into another century.

Now let's visit West Edmonton Mall, a shopping and entertainment centre with 800 stores, services and seven theme parks under one roof. Wow! West Edmonton Mall is grand and so is Edmonton with the other covered malls, Rexal Place and Commonwealth Stadium.

Edmonton, Edmonton you are okay, having celebrated more than one-hundred years as a city of champions, marching, marching strong and free into another century.

Edmonton with plenty of sunshine and a blue sky has a river valley filled with numerous parks and golf courses. Across the North Saskatchewan River is Old Strathcona with numerous unique shops one must visit. Edmonton in my arms I hold your charms beneath the skyscrapers above.

Edmonton, Edmonton you are okay, having celebrated one-hundred years as a city of champion, marching, marching strong and free into another century.

We take our education seriously with universities of Alberta and Grant MacEwant along with NAIT and the other colleges. And we are proud of our libraries and health care facilities. Come with me and I'll take you through The University of Alberta, Royal Alexandra and Misercordia to name a few. Capital Health we are proud of you.

Edmonton, Edmonton you a okay, having celebrated one-hundred years as city of champions, marching, marching strong and free into anther century.

of a cigarette or have I found a blanket, towel,
Bible in a suitcase.

I found whisky rings staining the desktop
bottle or a television busted or the remote
ing. And I never missed a key to a room at
e. Certainly your pet dog is welcome to stay

g will vouch for your parents, bring them

el MacDonald Manager

rom Calgary to Edmonton is approximately
one drives straight north along Queen
hway #2. It's not as far as Grande Prairie
n Red Deer.

arrived at majestic Fairmont Hotel
a Friday night, registered and before going
for a swim in the hotel swimming pool.
were three pools at the Mac – one filled
er, the second with cool water and the third

the receptionist, "Why the empty pool?"
replied, "Simple. Many customers who
ton and stay at the hotel can't swim."

nd part of Sunday the Remus's toured
West Edmonton Mall and took in a Paul
t Rexall Place.

Edmonton is the capital of Alberta and winner of numerous
international championships in basketball, figure skating,
curling, baseball, football and hockey. We are proud of the
Eskimo's winning the Grey and the Oiler's the Stanley
Cups. Edmonton is also the home of the Canadian Rodeo
finals, the Fringe, Folk and Heritage festivals and Capital
EX exhibition.

Edmonton, Edmonton you are okay, having celebrated
one-hundred years as a city of champions, marching,
marching strong and free into another century.

Edmonton is a gateway to the North where diamonds, oil
and natural gas are abundant.
And don't forget our nearby agricultural farm land and
product it produces.. And my dear friend, a meal isn't a
meal until you taste Alberta beef.

Edmonton, Edmonton you are okay having celebrated
one-hundred years as a city of champions, marching,
marching strong and free into another century.

Edmonton you are my city, my love. From the time of the
stagecoach to the LRT, and now the latest technology,
you have expanded through the decades. You are a city
of excellence, a host to the world and having celebrated
a century. May God guide you through the next one-
hundred years.

Edmonton, Edmonton you are okay, having celebrated
one-hundred years as a city of champions, marching,
marching strong and free into another century.
E D M O N T ON!

WHAT IS A HOME

A home is a place of residence or refuge and comfort built on a piece of land. It is usually a place in which an individual or a family live and able to store personal property. Most modern day households contain sanitary facilities and a means of preparing food. An individual may relate to a mental or an emotional state of refuge, comfort and privacy. A modern home is a place where a switch controls everything except the kids, and it has gadgets to do everything except make the mortgage payments. A home is more than that, it a place where one can worship, study, relax and enjoy warmth, comradeship and happiness.

PR

FIC

Joe and Marge Ren
Ed lived in Calgary
watch the Flames p
League game. Wond
weekend Ed's fathe
next weekend?"
While having brea
suggested, "Let's
economic oil boom
flocking to the Cit
real estate market
Ed's parents agre
"First however, w
will accommod
suggested and as
several days the
wrote back:

Dear Ed Remus
I have manage
had to call the
small hours of

fire because
glasses or a
Never have
from a dog'
control miss
checkout tin
at the Mac.
PS: If the d
too.

J. M. Swintak
Fairmont Hot

The distance
180 miles as
Elizabeth Hig
but further th

The Remus's
MacDonald on
to sleep went
Actually there
with warm wat
was empty.

When Ed asked
she graciously
come to Edmor

That Saturday
the city, visited
Brandt concert

On Sunday evening the Remus's returned to Calgary and Ed's close friend, Sammy Helper, asked what Edmonton was like.

In reply Ed said, "The city is littered with cranes. There's a building boom. Eventually I would like to live there and become a real estate salesman."

To accommodate his son Ed's father got a transfer of employment as a senior oil company executive from Calgary to Edmonton and listed the Remus home for sale with a realtor.

After the listing expired and they tried to sell the home independently by inserting ads in newspapers and on shopping mall bulletin boards Ed said, "Dad, let me try to sell our home."

"Go ahead try," his father said and the following day Ed marched in the July Calgary Stampede Parade through downtown Calgary. Ed used creative showmanship by wearing a Raggedy Ann costume which was used for Halloween, advertising the home on a sandwich board. The spray-painted sign read: FOR SALE BY OWER A BEAUTIFUL HOME. Ed accidentally misspelled the word Owner in the FISBO (for Sale by Owner) sign. At the bottom were the address and phone number.

By the time the Stampede was over Ed's mother said, "Ed, this is like a zoo. My head is spinning. People are looking at our house every day."

That particular day two prospects were touring the upstairs, two more downstairs and another three waiting in the living room for their turn.

Like many home owners Joe and Marge Remus were doing it by themselves without a real estate agent hoping to avoid an agent fee that would cut several thousand dollars of their profit. But while selling their home in

Calgary they had to buy one in Edmonton. The payoff was that within a week the Remus's received a fair offer with a deposit but before they felt like prisoners in their own home constantly fielding phone calls, giving directions and tours. Prospects would call for an appointment only with the caller say, "We are standing outside in the driveway. Can we see your home now?"
These calls came even if it was already dark outside.

Troublesome as it may have seemed Ed decided then and there to become a real estate salesman and sent for an application form through his sponsor Best Realty Ltd.in Edmonton. Within a week Ed received a reply asking Ed to answer the following question:
'In order to become a salesman with our company – Are there any significant experiences you have had or accomplishments you have realized which will help you to become a successful realtor?'

In essay form Ed wrote back:

Dear Mr. Best:
I helped my parents to sell our home by using a sandwich board. I'm visionary and eventually hope to sell real estate on the moon. I'm a dynamic figure and often seen playing street hockey. The Calgary Flames are scouting me. In baseball I bat .230 and scouted by the Toronto Blue Jays. While fishing I always catch my limit. I enjoy playing golf. Unfortunately I can't swim but eventually intend to take lessons.

When I'm bored I turn hydrogen and oxygen atoms into water. The laws of physics do not apply to me. I'm an abstract artist, a philosopher and can read a whole book during recess. I'm fashion conscious and wear black stockings while in public.

I do not perspire or shave and have a haircut once a month. People trust me. I know the exact location of every shopping mall in Calgary and Edmonton.

I balance, I weave, I dodge. I frolic and have my own skate board, bicycle, credit card, driver's license and cell phone. All my bills are paid. On weekends I let off steam by going to concerts. I enjoy listening to Anne Murray, Jann Arden and Michael Buble. I enjoy politics too and have met and spoke to Prime Minister Stephen Harper who lives in Calgary. I translate documents into Pig Latin and wow women with my guitar playing. I manage time effectively. Using a .22 caliber rifle I recently shot 13 gophers on a farmer's field near Airdrie. I believe in Santa Claus, prayer, reincarnation and angels and saints. I'm a member of the No Name Universal Church where a 7th son of a 7th son taught me about honesty and corruption. I possess a slightly twisted, sarcastic and cynical sense of humor. That's me, Ed Remus, in a nutshell graduating from High School soon.

Within a week Ed's application was approved subject to him finishing High School and then writing an Edmonton Real Estate Board exam.

Following a successful garage sale the Remus's moved to Edmonton and purchased a home in the Glenora district which they thought was a piece of cake. To assist in the purchase Ed's father called on a realtor of Chinese heritage, Helen Yip, at Best Realty. After qualifying the Remus's Ms Yip said, "I'm going to match you and your home by using the ancient Chinese method *feng shui* method."

Ms Yip convinced the Remus's to buy an older type house in the Glenora subdivision.

There are things you should know about this particular house and it has nothing to do with an ancient Chinese ritual.

The house appeared like any ordinary three bedroom, white colored, bungalow with a picture window but after the purchase was made the Remus's discovered that they had made several mistakes:

(1) They shopped for a house without getting a pre-arranged mortgage. (2) Chose a lender based only on the interest rate forgetting about a balloon clause, and (3) Purchased the house without being professionally inspected.

After the Remus's moved into the house they went through an exhilarating experience of renovating it. The best way to start they thought, was to purchase several home improvement magazines, read through the articles and get useful tips. The first tip Joe Remus picked up was to have a large bank account, and the second, go to garage, liquidation sales and flea markets to purchase tools, lumber and paint.

Home renovating brought both joy and frustration and began with removing old fixtures, windows, tearing out door frames and drywalls, tonguing and grooving.

Of course everything did not go perfectly. Murphy's Law took its toll. Rain did not stop, the plumber broke his arm and the electrician fried himself while drilling through a wall. Renovation also revealed old termite damage, dry rot and the duct work was out of whack. There were glitches to numerous to mention and of course, plenty of cussing.

In the end of the renovation process there were enough changes made in the ecological picture that it's a wonder why the Edmonton City Council hadn't asked for an environmental impact statement.

During the month of June, the Remus family was sitting in the auditorium of the Ross Shepherd High School. Ed was graduating from grade twelve and growing into adulthood. To this point in life Ed had many pluses aside helping his parents to sell their home in Calgary. Ed also had the distinction of being the only High School graduate in Canada to write his English exam in Pig Latin believing PL should be Canada's third official language.
Ed had a look of maturity as the principal presented him with a diploma and said, "Ed Remus, congratulations. Now get rid of all the negatives and reach for the sky. The world is yours. Go and conquer it."

As soon as the graduation ceremony was over it wasn't certain if Ed, this five foot ten, 160-pound, athletic-looking teenager would be arrested when he picked up several of his class mates, cranked up the radio to full volume, and they were hollering and whooping, screaming and burning rubber in the family car on Jasper Avenue. Ed's parents were concerned that their only son wouldn't drive sensibly along Highway #16 to a grad bush party. Fortunately Ed did drive carefully and wasn't picked up by the cops but next day slept until noon and had the worst headache of his life when he reviewed copies of previous real estate exams at the Best Realty Ltd. office.

When the owner-agent George Best, took samples of previous exams one of the assignments was to write a short composition, which included a murder, real estate history and a mystery.

Ed on a piece of paper wrote: "Holy Moses, in the castle, the queen got pregnant. I wonder who did it."

The exam paper also asked candidates entering the real estate profession to write a short composition what each candidate would do if he/she earned a million dollars in commission. While other candidates wrote furiously Ed instead of writing, gazed out the window and handed in a blank sheet.

"Why Ed?" Best said looking at the sheet of paper. "You've done nothing. Why is that?"

"Well," Ed replied, "That's what I would do if I made a million dollars in commission."

The following week when Ed opened the envelope containing the actual exam he was nervous and when the first question asked, "In what part of Canada do most ignorant people live?" Ed wrote down 'Toronto', reasoning that according to geography the population of Toronto was densest in all of Canada.

In order to pass his exam Ed had to answer correctly other questions too such as:

1. Give the important characteristics of the ancient Babylonian Empire with particular reference to real estate.

2. What kind of a room is not found in a house? If your answer is mushroom draw a   sketch of one.

3. Why are they called apartments when they are all stuck together?

4. The statement: A realtor specializes in fabricated homes. Does that mean his/her sales are built on lies? If your answer is yes, write down in one or two sentences the greatest lie ever told. And please don't put down what a politician promises.

5. What is the difference between an Agent, Broker and a Realtor?

6. What kind of a house weighs the least? If your answer is a lighthouse, spell out the word ten times.

7. Explain the theory of supply and demand as it relates to real estate.

8. How has the war in Iraq and Afghanistan affected the world economic growth?

9. Where is the basement located in a three-story building?

10. Besides a vacuum cleaner, fly paper and a pooper-scooper, write down what you think is another collective noun.

Ed began writing furiously, first answering the above questions, then the Essay ones, followed by Multiple Choice and finally True or False. Among the True and False questions Ed had to decide if:

1. Market value is found only at a Farmer's Market?

2. A contract for sale of real estate property is not valid if completed and signed on the day of a barmitsva?

3. Objective Value is found only at Wal-Mart.

4. A Bundle of Rights includes the right to slug a realtor on the head if one isn't   satisfied with his/her service?

5. When the Legislature passes a Rent Control Act, it's an Act of God?

6. The effect of Condition Precedent is an extreme headache?

7. The highest or absolute value right in real estate is Fe Simple?

8. A counter offer is generally made on a kitchen counter?

9. A painting of Mickey Mouse is considered a chattel?

10. Loss of value to a building is due to any cause known as graphite vandalism?

Ed also had to pick the right answer in a series of 50 Multiple Questions. Here are copies of ten

1. The basic distinction between a salesman and an agent are:
   (a) The agent must have a bald head
   (b) The agent usually is older than the salesman
   (c) The agent is responsible to the vendor

2. Which of the following is a designation that can apply to people who have completed a prescribed course of studies in the real estate profession?
   (a) MLS,
   (b) FRI
   (c) CHMS
   (d) CBC

3. Under Alberta law a person under 18 years if age is considered:
   (a) An infant
   (b) an adult
   (c) a juvenile

4. What percentage of land in Canada is not considered arable?
   (a) 8%
   (b) 92%
   (c) 88%

5. When an agreement for sale is granted the title is held by:
   (a) Vendor
   (b) municipal office
   (c) purchaser's wife

6. A hip roof slopes:
   (a) Towards Mecca
   (b) Towards the North Pole
   (c) Four sides

7. If the mortgage provides that it may be paid out at any time without notice or bonus, the mortgage usually called:
   (a) A swear word
   (b) Open mortgage
   (c) Closed mortgage

8. When accepting a deposit on a real estate transaction it is payable to:
   (a) Revenue Canada
   (b) The Vendor
   (c) The agent

9. Canada's economy is considered:
    (a) Mixed economy
    (b) Gone to pot
    (c) Controlled by Ontario and Quebec

10. In event the purchaser does not fulfill the terms
    of an accepted offer the deposit is:
    (a) Used by the salesman
    (b) Forfeited to the vendor
    (c) Given to the Salvation Army

RATINGS

(a) 45 out of 50 - You may get your license
(b) 45 to 35- Have another exam within 2 weeks
(c) Less than 35 - Find yourself another profession

As soon as Ed completed writing his exam he turned it in to the supervisor and then went home to wait for the results and read books that dealt with real estate matters, and also watch videos on the same subject. The ten books Ed enjoyed reading the most were:

1. How to be a Superstar in Real Estate by author
    I. M. Wealthy
2. Amusing Incidents While Listing Homes by
    Mini Haha
3. Chattel or Fixture? by R. U. Upjohn
4. Real Estate as an Investment by Fun E.
    Humor
5. Diary of a Slumlord by Slum Lord
6. The Strength of the Canadian Dollar by More
    Cents
7. Strike it rich in real estate by Jack Pott
8. How to Save a Listing by Less Chance
9. Sue for Damages by I. M. Harsh

   10. Recession in the Real Estate Industry by Shirley Blue

Among he videos Ed enjoyed were:

1. Real Estate in Cyberspace produced by Clare Voyant
2. Real Estate in Saskatchewan produced by Ho Hum
3. Real Estate and the Environment produced by Les Waste
4. Real Estate for Dummies produced by R. U. Wise
5. Foreign Contract Workers produced by May Helper
6. Real Estate Humour produced by Marc Haha
7. Sophisticate City Living produced by Noy C. Barr
8. Unusual Real Estate Features produced by Joe. Joker
9. Deceptive Appearance produced by Luke Terrible
10. One-Of-A-Kind produced by Les Sinn

CHAPTER 1

As soon as Ed was notified he had passed his exam he joined the sales force at Best Realty. As Ed began his orientation he sat down at a table with the company owner and agent George Best. The two discussed various aspects of listing, selling and giving a house an edge on the market.

"Before a prospect arrives at a house he/she wants to see put several drops of vanilla extract in the oven and crank up the heat," Best suggested. Several other tips Best suggested for those putting there homes for sale are:

1. Replace the light bulbs with higher voltage.
2. Remove any items in the house that may create a junkyard image.
3. Place freshly cut flowers in the kitchen and living room.
4. Tidy up the garage.
5. Make certain the toilet is flushed in case the prospect wants to use it.

Ed then took a memory improvement course to enforce his knowledge. The course included parts on how to list properties, how to qualify a prospect; appraise a property and real estate language. Technical jargon in any profession can create confusion and misunderstanding for those not well versed in the lingo. The real estate profession is not an exception. The following are commonly used real estate industry terms along with plain English what Ed invented they could mean.

WORDS	WHAT ED THOUGHT THE WORDS MEANT
Abstract	First to add and then to subtract
Accord	A car cheaper than a Mercedes
Agency	A home for the aged
Agreement for Sale	A friend agrees to sail a boat
Appraisal	Another name for an umbrella
Block	A derogatory reference to a buyer or seller's head
Caveat Emptor	A Roman emperor
Chattel	Another name for a telephone company
Circuit Breaker	A purchaser who goes directly to the seller, bypassing a real estate salesman
Contract	To make smaller
Covenant	A home for nuns
Creditor	A member of the Social Credit Party
Cul-de-sac	A bag with shredded documents
Deed	Not alive
Deposit	Something you make in the bathroom
Fixed assets	People embedded in cement
In testate	In United States

Lease	Please
Lien	A popular girls name
Listing	About to go under
Mortgage	A dead male (French)
Mortgagee	A dead female (French)
Multiple listing	More than one ship gone under
Power of Attorney	Having a big mouth
Principle	A top honcho at a school
B. S.	Better Service
CEO	Chief Embezzlement Officer
CFO	Corporate Fraud Officer
SRA	Satanic Ritual Abuse
Financial Planner	A guy whose phone has been disconnected
Market Correction	The day after you buy stocks
Cash Flow	The time your cash goes down the toilet
Yahoo	What you yell after completing a successful real estate deal
Window	A place you jumped through after your deal collapses
Profit	An archaic word seldom used
Real estate broker	A real estate salesman who is broke most of the time
Realtor	A real person from Toronto
Closing statement	Thank God.

When it came to advertising Ed thought for example that *split* meant a home that was falling apart. *One of a kind* meant a cave with inside plumbing. *Reduced* meant either a house with bad tenants or one ideal for pygmies and, *Old Word Charm* meant no bathroom.

Ed did not realize *Spacious Green Grass* meant the septic tank had to be changed. *Country Living* could mean India or Rwanda. *Room to Grow* meant the house had 12-foot ceilings and. *Low Maintenance* meant no landscaping or grass. *Park-like Setting,* there's a tree in the back yard. *Natural Setting*, a deer or an elk will eat anything you plant. And, *Much, Much More*, meant can't think of anything else to say about the heap.

Bedroom Community, neighbor's gossip mach so one might as well invite them into your bedroom. *Deal Won't Last*, the house is collapsing. *Wide Open Floor Plan*, previous owners removed the supporting walls. *Hidden Away*, shrubs are so tall one can't see out the front window. *Secluded Setting,* far from anything convenient. *Rustic Charm*, house needs major structural repairs, and, *Handyman's Special*, another way of saying "disgusting," "rotten," "hopeless."

Unusual Features, the house has no roof. *Rare Opportunity to Buy*, No one wants it. *Asking Price*, Amount set on the property that a realtor thinks is too high, vendor thinks the price is to low and the prospect thinks the property isn't worth half the selling price.

Ed also memorized catch phrases he could use while overcoming objections, when handling indecisions, while trying to list FISBO's and qualifying prospects. He also joined the Best Realty salesmen in role playing and acted out a scene where a grasshopper kept jumping from place to place while an ant kept building a nest and saved.

Best also suggested Ed familiarize himself with economics and the routine of other salesmen employed by Best Realty but the latter wasn't a good suggestion because five salesmen: Jim Crook, Freddy Bandit, Bob Pickles, Eric Swindler and Elmer Cheat had unlikely surnames for a realtor and they spent much of their time enjoying themselves at a local watering hole. There was also Bob Sled but he was totally retired and active only every four years – during the Winter Olympics.

As for real estate economics Ed discovered that:
(1) You can talk about money without ever having to make any
(2) You can say "trickle down" with a straight face
(3) When you are in the unemployment line, at least you will know why you are there
(4) If you rearrange the word ECONOMICS, you get COMIC NOSE
(5) Mick Jagger and Arnold Schwarzenegger both studied economics and look how they turned out.
(6) Standard and Poor - your life in a nutshell
(7) Bear Market - A 6 to 19 month period when the kids get no allowance, the wife gets no jewelry
(8) Bull Market - A random market movement causing an investor to mistake himself for a financial genius
(9) Stock Split - When your ex-wife and her lawyer split you assets equally between themselves
(10) Institutional Investor - An investor locked up in a nuthouse

Ed also reviewed the Edmonton Real Estate Board forms and personal data sheet and signed both. He then joined the Alberta Real Estate Association, which automatically entitled him to use he word *Realtor* as his occupation aside from salesman.

He pledged to abide by the Board's and Association's bylaws, covenants, undertakings, waivers claims and live up to a code of ethics.

Ed next studied how to make a market analysis, prices of properties which sold in Edmonton during the past three months, what a pro forma was and the proper way to conduct Open Houses. This done Ed discussed house hunting by prospects and about housing styles, floor plans, square footages, zoning, demographics, community leagues and neighborhoods. All had to do with determining how happy home buyers will be in a house he/she picks out.

Best also reminded Ed that a salesman in order o be successful should be able to field questions from prospects about transit zones, schools, parks, churches, shopping malls, medical facilities and a neighborhood." All told they can be the determining point for a home buyer," Best said. "Often its amenities and distance to work or a combination of both that make the buyer choose one area over another."

Best went on to say that local people often have certain areas in mind as to where they want to live. But first-time buyers and people from out of town frequently need direction.

Realtors should be adept to asking leading questions to determine what are important to the prospect and where those needs can be met." It's not unusual for realtors to have first-hand knowledge of the area

Where a kid can play hockey, soccer or baseball or how far it's from a shopping mall and a church". Best then gave

Ed a piece of advice, "A school site doesn't mean a school will be built there."

Ed then was given a pair of grey-colored slacks, a blue jacket with a Best Realty crest on it, a matching necktie and a pair of black-colored socks. Why black socks?"
Because Ed was a fashion trendsetter. Black looks dressy and doesn't show dirt.
Even while attending High School Ed conducted an experiment during a science class where three rats wore different colored socks: black, white and red, and then posed the same question to his classmates: "Which colored socks look the best?"
Ed continued with his experiment a week later when he took the three rats to the annual meeting of the Alberta Real Estate Association held in Edmonton and placed them on a table. To the agents and salesmen he posed the question, "If you were inclined to hire a rookie salesperson which colored socks would you like him/her wearing?"
The answer was unanimous: "A salesman with black socks or pantyhose."

As soon as Ed was outfitted with a suit of clothing he was told during his first day of orientation to make cold calls and see if he could pick up his first listing. Ed recalled what the High School principal said on graduation day: "Get rid of the negatives. Reach for the sky. The world is yours. Go and conquer it!"

Initially Ed teamed up with Mr. Best and the two chose an area in the Glenora district where a lot of pensioners lived. They walked from house to house making cold calls and telling the occupants that since Edmonton was booming it was a seller's market.

At the first call Best, who had 20 years experience as a realtor, said to the owner, "You should sell you home now while the market is hot. In addition to the hot market it appears to me that you are a heavy smoker and statistics indicate may die of cancer soon."

On the way to the second home Best said, "Ed, while making a pitch for a listing a realtor has to be observant and watch for clues on what subject to talk about initially and get the prospect motivated. For example at the last home, there were cigarette ashtrays and the odor of tobacco smoke."

"I got you," Ed said and when it was his turn to approach a prospect he said to the lady of the house, "Madam, you have to cut down on your cholesterol level and stop drinking milk and eating butter and cheese."

As the two realtors were on their way to the third home Best congratulated the rookie real estate salesman and said, "Ed, that was excellent but tell me, what did you use for a clue to initiate a conversation?"

Simple," Ed replied, "The milkman hiding under the woman's bed."

Ed enjoyed doing cold calls and evaluating homes. Some of the reasons were:

- He could dazzle his friends with his knowledge of external obsolescence
- He could see the wonderful world of pigeons, mice, bats and spiders
- See spaces in people's houses that usually required a search warrant
- Take notice that some people still do hang on their living room walls portraits of Elvis Presley, Marilyn Monroe and Pope John Paul 11.

- Get attention in the neighborhood while walking around with a clip board

Next day Ed went searching for a listing alone where at one home a young boy answered the door and Ed said, "Hello, may I speak to your daddy or mummy."

The youngster replied, "They're not home."

"Well is there anyone else I can talk with?"

"Would you like to speak to my sister?"

"Please,"

The boy went away and returned a minute later, "Mister."

"Yes,"

"I can't lift my sister from the play pen."

"That's all right I'll phone your dad later."

And when Ed did his first question was, "Are your mom or dad home yet?"

"No, sir."

"Can I leave a message?"

"You sure can mister, wait till I find a pencil."

Ed waited and when the youngster returned said, "Mister."

"Yes."

"I'm here but you want to know something?"

"What?"

"I can't write only print."

Frustrated Ed never did talk to the boy's father until much later.

On the same day Ed got his first listing and was trying to figure out how to measure a flagpole in front of the house. Ed got a ladder and a tape measure and went up to the flagpole. However the measurement turned more difficult than he had expected when both the tape measure and the ladder fell to the ground. The whole thing tuned into a disaster. Frustrated Ed phone Best at the office explaining what had happened.

Best shook his head and said, "Pull the flagpole out of the ground, lay it on the grass and then measure it from end to end."

After Ed hung up the receiver he said to himself, "I'm looking for the height of the pole and he gives me instructions on how to find the length."

Ed eventually did measure the pole.

The following day Ed put on his skate board and while working alone came upon a home that was partially destroyed, valuables stolen and furniture ruined. Vandals had broken into the home before the owners returned home from a holiday in Mexico. Seeing Ed the husband said, "Vandals stuffed the drains with their socks and then turned on the taps."

Upon inspection Ed could see the ceiling collapsing and when he entered the sunken living room he was up to his ankles in water. The couple managed to salvage some of the clothes but the photos of their children were lost for ever.

To make the damage more catastrophic the culprits spray-painted the walls and plumbing fixtures. Only the outside walls of the house and its foundation were salvageable. "It gives me the creeps to walk into our home. Luckily were are covered with insurance," the wife said as her husbanded turned to Ed and continued, "Would you like to list this place for sale? While Ed was making up his mind the wife said, "Sight on scene".

At the next stop a newly wed couple's home turned into a nightmare after the fried and groom had discovered that the home they had purchased a month earlier had been the scene of a grisly murder. The couple was horrified that in the FOR SALE BY OWNER home the owner's wife had been murdered by a prospect, the body chopped into pieces and thrown into a back ally dumpster. The newly married couple was upset and reluctant to move in.

"Even our mom's say they won't come to visit us if we move in," the bride said.

"Tell me more."

The groom took over. "It was a week ago that we found out about the murder. The fact that the murder took place in the home we bought is a latent defect and it should have been disclosed by the owner at the time we signed the purchase agreement."

"That will teach you to buy a home through a FOR SALE BY OWNER sign Ed thought but used good judgment and instead said, "So you want to list the home for sale through me?"

"No we already spent $5,000 in renovating the place. All we want is advice on what to do?" the groom continued.

"My advice is find yourself a lawyer who specializes in real estate matters," Ed said and while continuing searching for more listings came to a home which was partially destroyed. Valuables stolen and furniture ruined. Vandals had broken into the home before the owners returned from a holiday in Mexico.

Seeing Ed with a clipboard the owner said, "The vandals stuffed the drains with clothing and tuned on the taps."

Upon inspection Ed could see that the ceiling was collapsing and when he entered the sunken living room he was up to his ankles in water. The couple managed to save some of the clothing but photos of their children were lost for ever. To make the damage more catastrophic the culprits spray painted the walls and plumbing fixtures. Only the outside walls of the house and the foundation was salvageable.

"It gives me the creeps to walk into our home." the owner continued. "Luckily we had insurance and would like you list this house for sale while we move into an apartment.

A week later Ed got another listing on a tiny older- two bedroom house on a large lot and the vendor, Frank Smith, made an offer on a larger three bedroom bungalow. The offer on the bungalow was subject to Smith selling his home within seven days. Ed evaluated the tiny home based on recent comparable sales in the area and then said to Smith, "Your home needs major repair. On the other hand one can never tell who is in the market for a home like yours that needs work."

"Work?" Smith said.

"Like the living room walls, the bathroom and the roof. Take a day or two to paint the interior and then I'll start bringing prospects."

Smith, his wife and their two daughters stayed up all night painting the kitchen and removing mildew from the bathroom tiles. Smith then installed a lovely toilet seat he had purchased earlier at a flea market for fifty cents.

On the second day the first potential buyers were secluded to arrive so Smith said to his two teenage daughters, "Listen, our home won't sell unless we impress the prospect with neatness. Your mother will tell you what that means."

"No more underwear left on the stairs or the floor of your bedroom," Mrs. Smith explained. "Or drops of toothpaste left in the bathroom sink. You will make your beds the moment you get up and no like down all day. Better still why don't you sleep on the floor in your sleeping bags so that the beds won't be messed up. Your father will have to smoke and take his naps in the garage as soon as he hauls the junk inside away."

At 11:00 a. m. Ed phoned to say that he was on his way with Mr. and Mrs. Steele. In that time the Smith's placed themselves in positions where one daughter stood in the living room, covering cigarette burns in the carpet. The second daughter stood near a window with her back against water stains on the wall.

Mrs. Smith meanwhile sprayed the entire house with a herbal scented air freshener. The two dogs were tied to a tree in the back yard which had come down with Dutch elm disease.
The Steele's inspection was so fast that Smith didn't have time to tell them that the house was only a block away from an oil company planning to build a service station across the street.

On the third day Ed phoned and said that the Ashton's were coming and, "Let's spread some leaves over the bare spots on the front lawn."
"That's an excellent idea," Smith replied and quickly led his wife and daughters with the camouflage. As soon as the Ashton's arrived at the front door a gust of wind blew the leaves away.
The Ashton's stayed longer than the Steele's but they hadn't found a dream home either although they had found yellow patches on the lawn.

On the fourth day Ed phoned and said, "Your home isn't
suitable for the Ashton's. They want something bigger
but loved the aroma of the air freshener so don't air the
place out
because I'm bringing the Actuel's. Hey, why don't you
light the fireplace so the home looks lived in?"
"I'll have the fireplace going by the time the Actuel's
arrive," Smith said.

The Actuel's arrived on schedule, equipped with a
measuring tape. Mrs. Actuel dropped to her knees and
began measuring the living room carpet which would be
replaced.
Mrs. Actuel was so engrossed in measuring that she didn't
notice smoke billowing from the fireplace. When she did
notice she said, "Hey, is the house on fire?"
Smith said the house would never catch on fire because it
was built mostly of concrete and brick."
The Actuel's seemed so gracious that Smith felt sorry he
could not help clear their lungs.

On the 5th day the phone rang again and Ed said to Smith,
"Forget the Actuel's, they made an offer on a larger house
with new carpets and a fireplace that did no send out
smoke signals."
"What are we going to do? We have only two days left
before the *subject to* clause is to be removed on the
bungalow? Smith asked.
"I'll tell you something."
"What?'
"Let's reduce the price by $5,000."
This time Smith did not say *'It's an excellent idea'* but
gave Ed permission to lower the price by $5,000. During
an Open House prospects came but no offer was made.

Most of the prospects that came to see the home said, "We're just looking."

By now Smith found his tiny home so attractive that he was inclined to take it off the market until it began to rain.

On the sixth day Ed arrived with Mr. and Mrs. Doyle but they didn't make an offer because their dream retirement home didn't mean taking a shower in the living room where the ceiling went drip, drip, drip. There was one consolation however; the Doyle's wouldn't have to water their plants.

As soon as the Doyle's left Smith crawled into the attic and patched the roof from inside with a silicone gun. On the way down he slipped off a beam and punched a hole in the ceiling. He immediately called a carpenter and pleaded, "We re trying to sell our home. Can you please repair the ceiling by midnight?"

The carpenter managed to repair the ceiling on time and when Ed phoned on the seventh day he said, "I'm bringing Ms Lakes at eleven o'clock."

"We are ready for her." Smith said. The ceiling and the roof have been fixed."

To Ms Lakes house hunting was as exciting as an Olympic event. Her enthusiasm for the house was filled with warmth, so much so, that Smith began to confess about its defects.

Smith was making his way to the repairs he had done when Ms Lakes made an unexpected offer which Smith accepted, and then, had the subject to clause removed on the offer he had made on a three bedroom bungalow in a another neighborhood

A week after the Smith's took possession of their home they drove by their former residence and were surprised that it had been demolished.

But that did not matter, what did, was that both Smith and Ms Lakes were satisfied customers and Ed made his first sale. Ms Lakes had the tiny home torn down so that she could build a larger one on the huge lot, which had a panoramic view a valley and the North Saskatchewan River flowing through the middle of the city.

The home-building project for Ms Lakes began with a bulldozer driving smack into the middle of the house. The sound of a bulldozer was music to Ms Lake's ears, as she said to anyone who questioned her, "I've been planning to build a custom-built home for months but couldn't find a large enough lot with a view"

Ms Lakes didn't salvage much from the house before it was torn down. She saved the antique bathtub, living room chandelier and the toilet seat, which she donated to the Edmonton Museum

The following day Ed kept an appointment with an elderly prospect that was unshaven and dressed in shabby clothing. The man's belt buckle sank 2 inches into his stomach and his black shoes and yellow jacket were in need of repair. Ed showed the prospect a low-priced home, a medium priced and finally a more expensive where he said to the prospect after viewing, "This home may be too expensive for you."

The prospect had a twinkle in his eyes as soon as Ed said, "Too expensive for you."

Believing there is no substitute for experience the prospect then asked Ed, "How long have you been selling real estate?"

In jest replied, "There's a little know fact about my career that Moses brought three tablets from the mountain. There were the Ten Commandments and the other was my real estate license."
The prospect then asked Ed if had sold a high-rise.
"I have."
"Please tell me about the experience."
"Well, I sold a high-rise in the middle of the city that was so tall one could touch the stars from a penthouse on top. One could also tickle the feet of angels as they flew by."
After pausing for several seconds the shabbily dressed prospect said. "You want to know something."
"What?"
"I have free advice for you."
"What kind of advice?"
"Never judge your prospect by the clothing he or she is wearing. You have underestimated my intelligence and that is why I will not by a house through you but through another salesman."

Ed talked himself out of a listing and the following day had difficulty in negotiating others. In the first a couple arrived in Edmonton and was trying to find an apartmerrt to rent which because of the boom was difficult to find. The couple was dismayed when Ed casually said, "Looks like there is anti-Semitism in Edmonton."
Confronting Ed the male prospect said, "So you don't want to help us with a rental because you think we are Jewish."

Ed thought with a name like Libowitch, who else might you be?" but did not say those words out loud.

"Well, test me," Libowitch persisted.

"Fine. I'll ask several questions. The first is: Who are members of the Trinity?"

"Father, son, spirit."

"Correct. Next question is, whom was Mary married to while on Planet Earth?"

"Everyone knows that. It was Joseph the carpenter."

"Correct. At the time of marriage how old was Mary?"

"Thirteen."

Ed continued, "Correct. Wise men followed the stars and brought gold, frankincense and myrrh to the child in Bethlehem. How many wise men were there?"

"The number isn't important. It's the symbolism the gifts represent that counts."

"True. Now the final question. Why was Jesus born in a stable next to the animals instead of a hospital or a five-star hotel?"

Libowitch smiled. "As a rabbi I know the answer. It was because long ago like the present, real estate salesmen wouldn't rent to Jews."

Ed did find a rental for Rabbi. Libowitch and then introduced him to Pastor Taylor of the No Name Universal Church and Father Ted McCarthy from the Perpetual Help Catholic parish.

Father McCarthy's church and Rabbi Libowitch's synagogue were across the street from each other, their schedules intertwine and since their parishioners weren't generous, they decided to pool their resources and buy a car. After they bought a used Chevy, they drove it home and parked it on the street between the two places of worship.

A few minutes later the Rabbi looked out the window and saw Father McCarthy sprinkling water on the car. It didn't need a wash so the rabbi ran out and asked Father Mac what he was doing.

"I'm blessing it."

Rabbi Libowitch said, "Oh", and ran back to the synagogue reappearing a few minutes later with a hacksaw, ran to the car and cut off the last two inches of the tailpipe. That did not bother Father McCarthy who said, "It's a perfect example of ecumenism."

The following week Ed and Rabbi Libowitch were golfing and at a spot where the next green was 200 yards away over numerous hazards. Rabbi Libowitch shut his eyes and took a lusty swing. By a freak of chance the Rabbi connected the ball and set it sailing for the green. The ball bounced directly into the cup for a hole in one.

"You made a hole in one. That was an unbelievable shot," Ed said.

"And I'll wager you that with God's help I can make another."

"Okay, "Ed groaned. "But on one condition.

"What's the condition?"

"This time that you can make the shot with your eyes open."

The two golfers came to a difficult par with a water trap by a tree. Ed proceeded to hit the ball which landed in the North Saskatchewan River. To retrieve it he simply approached the water and extended his club .Ed took another shot and the ball landed on the green.

Rabbi Libowitch too hit the ball directly into the river where it quickly began to sink. As the ball was sinking, a fish grabbed the ball in its mouth. At that very moment an eagle plucked the fish out of the water and began carrying it aloft. As the eagle soared higher and higher, a bolt of lightning startled the bird which dropped the fish into a nearby tree when the fish struck its branch, the ball popped out, rolled across the green and into the cup for another hole in one,

Although Ed believed in angels and saints he grunted, "Rabbi Libowitch I hate golfing with you."

Ed had a good rapport with the local clergy in hopes that eventfully they would provide
him with leads

The following weekend Ed took Reverend Taylor duck hunting and bragged how he shot 13 gophers in Airdrie.
"Every time I pointed a gun a gopher fell to the ground."

Ed and Pastor Taylor of the No Name Universal Church dug a hole in the morning and waited. Soon a lone duck flew by. Ed pointed the gun into the air, fired several shots but the duck kept flying.
"Hey. Ed," Pastor Taylor said. "I thought you said that every time you pointed a gun into the air a duck would fall to the ground."
"I did say that," Ed replied. "This phenomenon is known as the Edmonton Miracle."
"An Edmonton Miracle, what is that?"
"A dead flying duck."
Ed and Pastor Taylor eventually did shoot several ducks.

On a week evening Ed took Father McCarthy to the Northlands Park horse races where the priest apparently blessed a horse with holy water. Following a similar blessing the horses won races 2, 3 and 4. Seeing this Ed placed his money on the next horse that Father McCarthy sprinkled with holy water but half-way around the track the horse fell and died.

That is when Ed said, "Look Father, I lost a bundle of money on the horse in the 5th race.

"Are you Catholic?" the priest asked politely.

"No, I'm a member of the No Name Universal Church."

"Ed," Father McCarthy replied, "If you were you would have won had you known the difference between a blessing and the last rites."

Father McCarthy enjoyed horse racing and since he was a clergyman from a poor parish asked Ed for suggestions as how he could raise money for the parish rectory which needed renovating. Ed responded by saying that Farmer Gartner in Spruce Grove was having a horse auction and he could personally enter a horse on the following race date. But Father McCarthy made a poor buy, instead of buying a horse he bought a donkey also known as an ass, and entered the animal during next race day. The donkey placed third.

The morning headline in the *Sun* read" *Father McCarthy's Ass Shows.*"

The archbishop saw the article in the newspaper and was greatly displeased. Next day the donkey placed first and the headline read: *Father McCarthy's Ass Out In Front.*

This time the archbishop was up in arms. Something had to be done. The donkey was entered in a race again and placed second and the newspaper headline read: *Father McCarthy's Ass Back in Place.*

That was too much for the archbishop, so he forbid Father McCarthy to enter the donkey in any more races.

The headline next day read: *Archbishop Scratches Father McCarthy's Ass.*

Finally the archbishop ordered Father McCarthy to get rid of the animal but he was unable to sell the donkey so he gave it to Sister Martha as a pet.

The archbishop ordered the nun to dispose the animal at once. She sold it on E-Bay for $10.

Next day the headline in a newspaper read: Sister Martha Peddles Her Ass for $10.

A week later a Black man, Gene Washington, made an offer through Ed on a house in a predominantly White subdivision.

The offer was subject to Washington obtaining a satisfactory mortgage through a bank but when Washington was interviewed the banker said, "With your income the bank may have to foreclose on you."

"So you do not want to approve a mortgage because of my income?"

"That's one reason."

"You mean to say there's another."

"If it came to foreclosure a White man would not buy your house."

"I have heard that before." Washington said.

"Heard what?"

"That the real estate value would depreciate if a Black man lives in a White neighborhood."

Washington eventually purchased a home in the outskirts of Edmonton by making a down payment and through an agreement for sale method.

Ed soon gained enough experience listing and selling that he was allowed to deal with international clients. Ed's first prospect was a financier from Hong Kong who was searching for a home to purchase. This occurred after Ed and the prospect Chung Lee, had drink of gin and tonic at the Westin Hotel bar. Ed had driven the multi-millionaire throughout Edmonton and came to a wonderful home beautifully landscaped overlooking the North Saskatchewan River.

Ed finally asked, "Well what you think of this fine piece of property?"

"I don't care for it. Take away the North Saskatchewan River and what have you got?"

Ed naturally was disappointed and on his way back to the hotel asked Lee what he thought of Canadian real estate salesmen?"

"You are funny people indeed."

"How did you reach that conclusion?"

"Simple. You take a glass, put sugar into it so it's sweet and a piece of lemon to make it sour. You put gin into the glass to make you warm, and ice to make it cool. And then you say 'Here's to you" and drink it yourself."

"It's the Canadian way."

"Canadians are funny people indeed,"Lee continued, I take a stroll down Jasper Avenue and see a sign that reads *Batchelor for Rent*. Moving on I stop at a grocery store for a pint of milk and find it strange that the advertisement on the package says *2%* or *Homo*. You Canadians are funny people indeed."

Not only did Ed have difficulty dealing with a Chinaman from Hong Kong but also with an Arab-speaking farmer near Spruce Grove, Mohammad Mohammad, who wanted to cash-in on the real estate hot market and sell his farm.

Through an interpreter Ed asked Mohammad how much his farm expected to yield that year. Mohammad responded by becoming exited and angry. In order to soften the reply the interpreter said, "Ed, he says he doesn't' know."
Ed realized something hand gone wrong but had no way knowing what. Later Ed learned that that Arabs regard anyone who tries to look to the *future* as slightly insane. When Ed asked about the future yield the Arab was highly insulted since he thought Ed considered him crazy. To an Arab only God knows the future and it's presumptuous to ask.

Ed had a different experience however, when he met with an executive representing a major oil company that was searching for sites for service station in the greater Edmonton area. The executive cross-examined Ed on the merits of various potential sites and finally said to Ed, "All right. I'll give you a letter of introduction to the CEO of our company whose office is in Calgary."
Ed met with the CE0 and got a $1-million order. In his zeal Ed forgot about the letter and did not present it. Back in Edmonton several days later Ed found the letter in his suit pocket. Curious he opened it. The instructions inside were, "Learn all you can from Mr. Remus but don't purchase any land through him if you can help it."

A month after the oil company purchased the Edmonton landmark it altered its architectural plans for the service station to include a restaurant and a car-wash thus needing more space. The company asked Ed to present a fair offer on the adjacent lot with an old brick house on it but Ed met an irresistible force in an 82-year old widow by the name of Clara Baker. Acting for an unidentified client Ed came to Mrs. Baker's door and in current terms made a fair offer on the property.

"I'm sorry but this house isn't for sale." Mrs. Baker said, "But please come in and have a cup of tea with me."

While having tea Ed indicated that the client may pay a bit more but Mrs. Baker shook her head and said, "Definitely not. My home isn't available for any price. It's part of my heritage and I intend to spend the rest of my life right here in my home."

Meanwhile the oil company applied for a building permit showing a service station, a restaurant and a car-wash and a large parking area.

Across the street residents signed a petition charging that the service station would congest local traffic, disturb the neighborhood peace and lower property value.

As a champion of commercial development Mayor Mandel called a special council meeting and after reading the petition cautioned his council members, "The service station means taxes and jobs. This is a progressive step council has to support otherwise the oil company will build its service station in Sherwood Park or Spruce Grove.

In reply Mrs. Baker spoke out in public for the first time and questioned the wisdom of ripping down a perfect old house with a historical background, during a housing shortage.

"In any case I won't sell my property to any one at any price," Mrs. Baker said.

Having gone public the oil company sent its own officials to talk to the elderly widow and they came in a pecking order: chief legal council, vice-president, chief executive officer, and then the presidents himself who flew in from Calgary and raise the company's ante to twice the market value of the property but to no avail.

Mrs. Baker insisted, "My old brick house is something money can not buy. The house embraces a bygone era and many memories I treasure."

The company president realized Mrs. Baker was a difficult nut to crack so he advised the company directors to back off from making additional offers.

For her part Mrs. Baker advised the president that the company could have first option on the house and said, "I have willed it to my son John and when I die you can negotiate with him."

In the meantime the oil company proceeded with construction of the service station minus the restaurant and Mrs. Baker paid dearly for this. Next to her house the building contractor worked behind a wire fence, and Mrs. Baker's quiet street echoed to the noise of a jackhammer and a bulldozer.

Pile drivers rattled her dishes and dust covered everything inside the house but Mrs. Baker was determined not to sell no matter what the problems meant. To relatives and friends she said, "Money has no match for a household of memories. That is why I now take sleeping pills to blot out the sound of the drills."

Three months later the Mayor officially opened the service station and those who came to fill of with gas watched the elderly Mrs. Baker as she sat on the front porch knit or crochet.

A month after the official opening E decoded to see Mrs. Baker if she had changed her mind about the house only to discover that she had died and the house where she lived was torn down and buried under tonnes of parking lot pavement.

Mrs. Baker was a hard nut to crack and so was her son John who after inheriting the money from the sale of the house applied for a zoning change to establish a used-car lot next to the service station which was in a semi-residential neighborhood.

The zoning change was opposed by a well organized Community League and the first thing that surprised Ed about the David vs. Goliath battle was that the activists managed to win sometimes. Faced with developers who can afford to pay high-priced lawyers to attend public meetings may be stressful because ordinary people often have to rustle up baby sitters and parking money in order to have their voices heard.

In this instance the Community League let John Baker know in no uncertain terms that neighbors in the area were going to make it difficult for any developer who threatened to eat up their quaint close-knit community with used cars.

City Council eventually turned down John Baker's application for a zoning change and the Mayor said, "To establish a used car lot on the proposed site would be Cultural Vandalism."

Ed's next experience in selling came when a Vancouver businessman arrived in Edmonton with the intent of starting a fish farm, Ed kept praising Edmonton as a community with substantial growth and a fish farm would be a welcome addition to its growth.

The Vancouverite eventually got tired of Ed praising Edmonton and said the only way he would invest in an aqua farm was if Edmonton was a sea port.

E burst out with laughter and asked the investor how Edmonton could become a seaport when it was a city in Canada's interior.

"Easy, one will have to build a pipeline to the Pacific Ocean."

"And then what?"

'And then Mr. Remus, if you can suck like you can blow Edmonton will become a sea port in no time."

Ed did not mind the putdown because an investor from Toronto was in search of property to open a *Subway* outlet.

Ed drove the prospect up and down Edmonton streets and when they drove past Rexal Place the Torontonian said Air Canada Place was in better shape and much larger .Then when they drove past Refinery Row and a gasoline storage tanks appeared the Torontonian asked, "What are these?"

"That's a row of salt and pepper shakers. Like the one's used at the Shaw Convention Centre."

"Unbelievable. Please drive me there."

Ed drove the Torontonian to the Shaw Convention Centre where a bartender placed a keg of beer in front of him.

Surprised the Torontonian said "I said a glass not a keg."

"Well," the bartender replied, "In Edmonton everything is huge, even bigger than in the state of Texas."

By this time the Torontonian had go to a public wash room and was told, "Down a few steps and then to the right."

As soon as the Torontonian left the bartender forgot to mention the swimming pool across from the washroom so he followed him. As the bartender approached the pool

the Torontonian was inside screaming, "Don't flush it! Don't flush it!"
The Torontonian turned out to be a flake. Ed however, gained experience as a tourist guide.

The oil and natural gas boom in Alberta was so rampant that even the Prince of Wales showed up in Edmonton to see if he could purchase land that was his criteria.
"I want something my children will have which I never had," the prince finally said as Ed led the search for that certain property.
After searching for a week Ed asked the prince, "Can you be more specific?"
"Yes, something similar to India."

Although Ed tried he could not find such a vast piece of land for sale.

When Ed asked the prince what he would like for his birthday the prince replied, "The province of Ontario."

Despite Ed's efforts to please the prince was a failure the following day he received a call to list a prefabricated house.
"Your home is beautiful but isn't it a bit small?" Ed said to the owner upon arrival.
"Because of the current hot real estate market it would ruin me financially to buy a larger one, as it is the house cost me over $150,000."
"That's a lot of money for a small house, isn't it?"
"I was in a hurry as I was about to get married so I sent it to Edmonton from Vancouver via courier.
Ed listed the prefab at what he thought was the prevailing fair market value.

Other Experiences Ed had as a real estate salesman:

Ed approached an unkempt house and the puzzled owner said, "I didn't send for a real estate salesman."
Ed's reply was, "True, but your neighbor did."

Howls of pain emerged from a bathroom of an Open House held by Ed on a Sunday. Those attending found a prospective buyer glued to the toilet seat. An ambulance crew managed to pry him from the seat which had been covered with glue by a practical joker who passed through the house earlier.

A prospect phoned Ed and gave him the requirements for a home on an acreage he wished to buy. "About five acres on a gently rolling fertile land with some of it forested, some suitable for cultivation with a pond or a stream through it. And it must have a view."
Ed listened with patience and when the prospect was finished said, "Sir, we deal with real estate and not fantasies."

Ed one day received a fax that read:
Realtor Ed
The siding on the house I purchased isn't cedar but fir
Was your LMS listing printed in error?

Ed called a plumber to repair a leaking faucet in a home he had just sold and went to get anther listing. When Ed returned five hours later he asked the plumber, "How is it going?"
"Fine," replied the plumber. "Since I saw you last, I taught a youngster to swim."

Ed was having lunch with another salesman discussing a dog the other salesman had purchased. The other salesman said, "The dog is half boxer and half bull and it cost me $1000."
Ed then asked, "Whit part is bull?"
The other salesman replied, "That part about the $1000."

Best Realty was holding a salesmen meeting when the personnel manager asked, "How many people do we employ broken down by sex?"
"Sir," Ed replied, "I think there aren't many. Liquor is more a problem with our company."

Initially Ed knew little about ranching and farming. While appraising a property Ed found several milk bottles in the barn and came shouting, "Sir, look, I found a cows nest."

A prospect was looking for a farm near Red Deer and asked Ed if there were any Triple 'A' farmers around.
"Triple 'A' Farmers? Who are they? Ed asked and was told, "Those who farm during April. May and June and spend rest of their time in Arizona."

Ed and a realtor from the state of Montana were discussing the difference between Canada and United States.
"I know the difference," Ed said.
"What is it? the American asked.
"United States at one time had a president name Johnny Cash and a vice-present Bob Hope. It seems to me that Canada has a prime minister, no cash and no hope."

Ed was listing a farm near the Rocky Mountains when he was chased up a tree by two grizzly bears. The bears shook the tree but nothing happened so they disappeared only to return with four other grizzlies. The six bears took turn turns in shaking the tree but still nothing happened. Frustrated that they couldn't shake Ed down the six bears disappeared. Several minutes later one bear returned accompanied by a beaver. As soon as the tree was cut down, a truck passed by and the driver rescued Ed.

Although Ed could not swim he was tremendous ice fisherman. On Pigeon Lake one day all Ed used was a hatchet, alarm clock and a hammer but no hook. Ed used the hatchet to make the hole in the ice and then placed the alarm clock next to it. When the fish came to see what time it was Ed would whack the fish with a hammer across their head and pull out the fish one after another.

Ed was passing through the nearby Cree Enoch Indian Reserve and was surprised to see a woman carry her child in front of her.
"How come she carries her baby in front of her instead of her back like other Cree women do?" Ed asked the band leader.

And was told, "Last year Charlene was in Australia. She saw a kangaroo which must have had an influence on her."

Ed was sitting next to a priest during a flight to Vancouver.
Curious Ed said, "Tell me Father, why do you wear your collar back to front?"
"Because I'm a father."

"My father is a father too and he doesn't wear his collar like that."

"Ah," said the priest. "But I'm a father to thousands."

"If that's the case, then maybe it's your trousers that you should be wearing back to front."

Ed and two other realtors were discussing the advance views of their respective churches.

"We are so modern," asserted the first, "We have a computer preparing the sermon each Sunday."

"That's nothing," said the second, "The church I attend uses a robot instead of a clergyman."

"Hold it, both of you;" said Ed, "You aren't even in the same league compared to the church I attend. We at the No Name Universal Church are so reformed that we can be closed on Sunday."

Sales or lack of therefore, sometimes is the fault of a salesperson. With the right training a real estate salesman can become a super-producer. Sales can also be affected by marketing. Poor marketing skills lead to low sales volume. Face to face marketing skills. are secondary importance's remembering that pressure selling relates to lack of prospects. A realtor should never feel that one has to make a sale in order to drive an expensive SUV and even to survive.

Marketing campaigns often underestimate customer attitudes, and overestimate a products appeal. The traditional marketing focuses only on products and benefits from the salesman's point of view.

This arcane form of marketing does not seek to solve or answer immediate and long-term concerns of individuals.

The paramount sales environment is one that is created and supported by an active marketing plan.

When marketing is driving the company's overall strategy, present customers are better served and satisfied, new doors open, former customers are reclaimed and sales personnel spend their time doing what they do best – making sales. One of the secrets is to nab an award or win a contest which lead to being recognized as a distinguished professional in the industry.

With that premise Best invited a motivational speaker from the University of Alberta who gave seminars for employees of General Motors, Pepsi and Visa to give his salesmen a pep talk that would leave competition in the dust. Professor Vernon Law, an expert in time management, used illustrations that Best Realty salesmen would never forget. He stood in front of a group at a seminar and began:

"Okay, time for a quiz," and set a one gallon, wide-mouth Mason jar on the table in front of him and brought out a dozen fist sized rocks carefully placing them, one at a time, in the jar. When the jar was filled to the top and no more rocks would fit inside, he asked, "In your opinion is the jar full?"

All the realtors said, "Yes."

Dr. Law replied, "Really?" reached under the table and pulled out a bucket of gravel. He dumped some into the jar, shook it, causing pieces to work themselves down into the spaces between the rocks.

Dr. Law asked the group one more time, "Is the jar full?"

This time one of the realtors said, "Probably not."

"Good," Dr. Law replied, reached under the table and brought a bucket of sand, which he dumped into the jar.

The sand went into spaces left between the rocks and the gravel and one more time asked the salesmen, "Is the jar full?"

"No," all the realtors answered.

Once again Dr. Law said, "Good," and took a pitcher of water, poured it until the jar was filled to the brim. He looked at the realtors and asked, "What is the point of this illustration?"

Ed raised his hand and said, "Sir, the point is, no matter how full your schedule is, if you try really hard, you can always fit more things in."

"No," Dr. Law said, "That's not the point. The truth this illustration teaches us is: If you don't put the big rocks first, you will never get them in at all. What are the Big Rocks in your life? Your children. Your loved ones. Your education. Your dreams. A worthy cause. Teaching or mentoring others. Doing things you love. Time for yourself. Your health."

And then he continued, "Remember to put these Big Rocks in fist or you will never let them in at all.

If you add gravel, sand and water in that order, then you will fill your life with little things to worry about that really don't matter, and you will never have the real quality time you need to spend on the big important stuff like the *rocks*.

So tonight or in the morning, when you are reflecting on this short story, ask yourself this question: What are the big rocks in my life? Then put them into the jar first."

After being a participant in the Dr. Law seminar Ed's lackadaisical attitude changed and he entered the Best Realty two-week *Get A Listing Contest*. Salesmen who got the most listings within a period of two weeks would win as first prize not a holiday in Disneyland or Hawaii but

$2,000 in cash and an overnight stay at the Oasis Motel in nearby Wetaskiwin.

Now that Ed had received several commission cheques he went in search of buying a car but when he stopped at the Champion City Used Car Lot the salesmen convinced him to

buy an ostrich instead which the lot accepted as a trade-in on a previous sale.

"Riding an ostrich during the high price of gasoline, is much cheaper and more fun than driving a used car," the salesman and continued, "An ostrich is capable of doing 65 kilometers an hour and has enough hair to make you comfortable during winter. The animal is sturdy and sure-footed and has good traction on snow and ice."

Observing the bird from the front, sides and rear Ed said, "Does it really work?"

"It does and when it comes to personal safety ostriches have been known to chase coyotes and kick them. An ostrich stops at red lights."

Ed was debating with himself when the salesmen asked. 'Ed, do you play golf?"

"I do."

"Then I have more good news. You can use the ostrich as a caddy."

You mean to say that an ostrich a can tell the difference between 3 and 5 irons?"

"That is still researched but would you like to try one?"

"I was going to ask if I could."

"Go ahead."

The salesman explained the commands "Gee" and Haw" Ed got on top of the large bird and took off to the West End of the city where on 142 street he stopped at a red light when a truck pulled up behind him and heard the driver say to his passenger, "Look at that jerk on top of the ostrich"

Ed was back at the used car lot within an hour where the salesmen asked, "What happened?"

"The Ostrich stopped at a red light but when a truck pulled up behind me and I heard the driver say to the passenger, 'Look at that jerk on top of an ostrich'"

"And?"

"I got off the big bird to see who was the jerk."

"And then?"

"The ostrich then ran away to the Valley Zoo and now is a friend of Alice the Elephant and other animals."

Ed did not buy the ostrich but was determined to find something cheap that he could ride in or on, and take advantage of the listing contest he had won. This time Ed decided to buy a horse from farmer Jerry Gartner who initially did not want to sell. "Prince doesn't look good but if you want him you can have him," the farmer said.

Ed bought the horse but the following day became disappointed when he returned the horse and said, "Gartner, you sold me a blind horse."

Gartner casually replied, "I told you the horse did not look good. This is a perfect example realtor's often say 'Buyer Beware'."

Ed purchased another horse instead and was on his way southward on highway 2 to Wetaskiwin to claim his prize as the top listing salesman at Best Realty for that particular two-week period.

Halfway to Wetaskiwin Ed and the horse came upon a vicious wind and sand storm which caused chaos. Even the International Airport was closed and prompted health warnings by Alberta Health Care and Wellness. The storm was so severe that when it ended a motorist found Ed's head sticking out the sand.

"Wait," said the traveler, "I'll get a shovel and dig you out."

"Better get a bulldozer because I'm sitting on top of a horse," Ed replied."

A cat skinner was called, a bulldozer arrived, Ed and the horse survived and both were on their way to Wetaskiwin again.

As soon as Ed reached the outskirts of Wetaskiwin he drove up to a Convenience Store and said to the owner, "I've passed through a severe sand storm an hour ago and my horse is thirsty. Please give him a bucket of your best water to quench his thirst." It took 24 bottles to fill the bucket and the horse was so thirsty that he drank it all.

"He's still thirsty. How about another six bottles?" Ed continued.

The horse drank the additional water and Ed asked the manager, "How much do I owe you?"

"Bottled water is almost as expensive as a litre of gasoline these days. Your bill is $30. I think however, a man who loves his horse so much deserves more water on the house."

The manager was surprised when said, "Who? Me? Can't you see I'm driving?"

Ed paid the bill and continued riding to Wetaskiwin town centre until they reached the Oasis Motel which isn't to grand or stuffy, where the food in the restaurant is good but not flashy and according to some sleep is possible only with the double glazed windows are closed firmly because the motel is located on a street which turns into a drag strip near midnight.

Ed made the horse comfortable for the night and he himself entered the motel, which recently was purchased by an investor from Switzerland, and management was ho-hum and a linguistic boo-boo sign at the reception desk read:

DEER GUESTS NOTICE

1. It's forbidden to steel towels in this motel. If you are not a person to do such things, please do not read this notice
2. Please keep your valuables at the front desk. If you keep them in your room we are not responsible
3. Please do not P in the swimming pool
4. Visitors are expected to complain at the front desk between 9 and 11 a. m.
5. You are invited to take advantage of the women who are employed to clean your room
6. Yodeling lessons are given daily. See front desk clerk
7. See our dress shop next door where you will find dresses suitable for street walking
8. Cold and Heat. If you want condition in your room, please yourself
9. Today's Special - No Ice Cream
10. We are pleased to announce that management has personally passed all water   served here.

Ed was given a key and a valet carried his suitcase to the second floor which rooms instead of having numbers had terms related to the oil and natural gas industry.

A name plate on Ed's room read *Dry Well Room* and the men and women public washrooms were marked *Absolute*

Filter and *Abnormal Events.* Ed did not know which was which until he noticed a male leave the room marked *Absolute Filter.*

As soon as Ed unpacked and had several cocktails in the bar although he could not swim he put on his bathing suit and went to the indoor swimming pool. Ten minutes later Ed made his blunder when the manager hollered, "Hey, Mr. Remus, you can't swim in our pool any longer!"
"Why so?" Ed hollered back.
Because I saw you pee in the pool."
"I'm certain other guests did the same."
"Could be but not from the diving board."

Ed went to his room and fell asleep hoping the manager would not scold him.
At precisely midnight however, the manager knocked on the door and in a loud voice said, "Mr. Remus, have you got a woman inside your room?"
"Definitely not," Ed said as he opened the door.
Seeing the door opened the manager as pre-arranged with George Best of Best Realty handed Ed an envelope containing $2000 and before leaving said "Congratulations Mr. Remus on winning the Best Realty Listing Contest. Enjoy your prize and stay at the Oasis."

A day later Ed returned to Edmonton and decided to invest his $2000 by purchasing a car so he returned to the Champion City Used Car Lot and was highly impressed with a relatively new model that a salesman was anxious to sell..
"This like brand new blue Ford was previously owned by a lady wearing tennis shoes. She drove it only several times.

"You will notice that there are only 3000 kilometers on the odometer. You'll find that this car is a great bargain. It's our special this week," the salesmen said.

Being a bit cautious Ed checked the name on the registration certificate and phoned the woman and told her what the salesman had said about the vehicle.

"The salesman told the truth," the woman said and went on, "I'm 63-years old and always wear tennis shoes when I drive.

"The 3000 kilometers on the odometer is the correct mileage. I have participated in stock car races and came second once and third twice and would have finished the last race except I blew the engine."

Needles to say Ed did not buy this particular car but went to No-Name Motors and purchased a 1993, four door and burgundy colored Buick Regal with custom wheels and tires and a lush interior of tan leather.

The salesman who sold the car said to Ed, "If you are easy on the throttle, steady on the gears, roll her over gently and she'll last you for years.

The Regal also featured a bumper sticker that read "Go Eskimos - Go Oilers" and a horn which when pushed did not go "toot, toot" but made the sound of a Canada goose flying north or south.

While enjoying a cookie Ed paid for the car, pulled on the choke and left the used car lot in a cloud of smoke.

Next on Ed's career agenda was to buy a condominium with 5% down and a 25 year mortgage on Jasper Avenue. The condo kitchen was a bit small but Ed had no intention of doing his own cooking.

As soon as Ed moved into his condo he conducted a month -to-month survey to determine why at tines Best Realty sales were not what they were expected to be. Here are the reasons.

January	People spent their cash during the Christmas holidays
February	All the best customers had gone either to Arizona, Mexico or Hawaii
March	Everyone preoccupied with Income Taxes
April	Unseasonably cold weather and people spent too much during the Easter holidays
May	Too much rain. Farmers depressed
June	Too many couples getting married. No money left after graduation
July	Heat has people down
August	Everybody away on vacation
September	Everybody back but broke. Need money for education
October	Clients waiting to see how autumn clearance sales turn out
November	First snow storm. Some upset with results in the municipal election
December	Customers too busy getting ready for Christmas. Credit card limit reached

The following day Ed sold a home to a Denis Bougie in Bonnyville and sent him flowers for the occasion which said, "Rest in Peace."

Bougie got angry and called Ed to complain. After he had informed Bougie of the obvious mistake and how angry he was, Ed apologetically said, "Sir. I'm really sorry for the mistake, but rather than getting angry you should imagine this: There's a funeral taking place in Bonnyville today and a man being buried has received flowers with a note saying, "Congratulations on you new home."

When it came to newspaper advertising Ed most of the time did his in the Sun. One day a prospect was looking for a home to purchase and picked up a page with Ed's listing in it.

The prospect phoned Ed that he had found a termite on the page and wanted to know if the termite meant good or bad luck. Ed replied by saying, "Finding a termite on my advertisement is neither good nor bad. The termite probably was checking out the ad to see who isn't advertising to sell their home so that it can go there a lead a life of undisturbed peace."

Another way of creative advertising wasn't a ringing success. It seems that Ed sent out too many ringy-dingies in the middle of the night. The call triggered by a sophisticated dialing machine, woke hundreds of Edmonton residents between 3:00 and 9::00 to ask sleeping residents if they would like to list their home or buy a new one.
Following a flood of phone calls to the Best Realty office Ed admitted that he had made a mistake by hitting a.m. instead of p.m. on the automatic dialing machine. Ed admitted too, following the blooper that Edmontonians did not appreciate this form of canvassing,

ONE YEAR LATER

CHAPTER 2

As a salesman Ed was doing relatively well, however, his parents suggested their charismatic son, his father's pride and mother's love, might be more successful if he were married. Reassuring his parents that he now had his own condominium with a mortgage that if one cared to live, just miss a payment, and a1993 Buick Regal car Ed now felt he could support a wife and took his parent's challenge seriously to find a true loving wife.

Ed's condo was on the 12th floor of a middle class district on Jasper Avenue where onlookers swell each Friday night to see drag racers hit a light pole. It's also an area where street people beg for money on every block corner. Ed's domineering mother however, worried about her son so much that she had to use herbal medicine to cure her ills. Also it was a time when the family doctor, Stan Hardy, warned that Ed's mother would die of heart failure should Ed not be married within a year. Ed did not want this to happen and soon discovered the vicissitudes of his fortune and his search for a wife would be full of hope, fear, exultation and disappointments.

To please his parents Ed agreed that marriage was the best and perhaps the only means of increasing his sales so he first met Carmen who he knew in High School but

Carmen was a recycling advocate and said, "Ed, I'll never marry again."

Carmen said that husband number one was an Air Canada pilot who fell in love with a flight attendant during a layover in Paris and never came home. Husband number two was a polygamist and presently serving time in prison and number three no longer wanted to be a male and decided to have a sexual realignment.

After several more rounds of phone calls Ed spoke to Mary but Mary did not want to latch on to man to fulfill her life nor did she want to change her single status. Mary told Ed about her experience of a dating service she used to find a beau.

"My first date was a truck driver who hardly could speak English and wanted to crawl into bed ten minutes after we met," she said.

Mary remained in single blessedness.

Next Ed dated Penelope a crush who he knew while attending High School and now lived in the same condo complex. But Penelope wasn't looking for a relationship where commitment was the key element although she went out with men occasionally. Penelope wasn't tired sleeping with a vibrator and an electric blanket. A mortgage and a couple of kids weren't on her agenda.

After several more tries for a relationship with women he personally knew Ed picked up a copy of the *Sun* and began reading the personal pages where men and women, and those in between, were hoping to find love, or at least compatibility, through the pages of a newspaper.

Some ads sounded funny, a few descriptive words provided comic relief. Others however, allowed a glimmer of insight into the lives of females whom loneliness had been excruciatingly painful and took to the newspapers as a last resort.

The *Sun* carried several success stories from the Cupids Diary page that advertising in a newspaper for a mate gets results. Ed's quest to find a mate continued. Here are several Sun success stories in a nutshell.

Felix and Nellie
Moments after Felix read the Cupid Diary page he met Nellie. A short time later a kicking horse injured Felix's face. Nellie stood by Frlix during reconstruction surgery when she said, "I do." They are happily married.

Adam and Michelle
The fun-loving couple fell in love in a pea garden after reading Cupid's Diary.
They were married eight months later and can't help but smile each time they pass through the produce section in Safeway.

Anthony and Allison
Anthony was a waiter at a local restaurant when he read the Sun. Next day Anthony got a tip of his life time when Allison a customer at one of the tables asked him for a date. Allison has since agreed to stand by his side for ever as his wife.

Dean and Linda
Linda didn't speak a word of English when Dean read the lovelorn page in the Sun and found his pen pal in the Philippines. But that did not stop them from falling in love and spending the next 33 years (and counting) together.

Robert and Vicky
Robert was a patient at the Royal Alex hospital when he read the Cupid Diary and a cute nurse was attending him. Robert was about to move to Calgary in a few days. But after just one date with this beautiful nurse they were destined to make their home in Edmonton.

Richard and Helen
In less than a week reading the *Sun* Richard and Helen met while skiing in Jasper. The couple courted and was married. Twenty-five years later they are living proof that whirlwind romances don't just work in movies.

Roger and Eileen
Robert was interviewing high school students for positions as summer research students.
Eileen was the interviewee that captured Richard's heart. Talk about a teacher's pet. Eileen is still at Robert's side after 24 years of marriage and four children.

Charles and Krista
Charles was in search of an apartment when he came upon one managed by Krista and advertised in the Sun. After six months being a tenant Charles married his landlord. Now Charles and Krista managed the apartment complex together.

After reading the endorsements and flipping several pages Ed thought, "Here's a capable housewife."
"Dear Prince,
If you have found my glass slipper and a professional, I'm your slim blond, 23-year old attractive Cinderella. Why don't you phone or write me."

Ed did phone and after meeting Cinderella decided she did not suit his criteria but maybe it was wishful thinking, the power of suggestion or sheer osmosis Alfa did but after several dates she dumped him. In a lengthy letter Alfa wrote:

Dear Ed,

I regret to inform that you have been eliminated from contention as Mr. Right. You are probably aware the competition for my affection has been exceedingly tough and dozens of well-qualified candidates as yourself also failed to make the cut. I will however, keep your name on file should an opening become available. So that you find better success in your future romantic endeavors, please allow me to offer the following reasons why you were disqualified.

Your surname Remus is objectionable. I can't imagine taking it, hyphening it or subject my children to it because the legendary twins Romulus and Remus were brought up by a female wolf and were friendly to each other as teenagers but when they became adults they fought among themselves. And before Romulus became king of Rome he murdered Remus. In your journey through life I'm afraid, you like the Remus long ago, will have a violent death and as you know funeral expenses are steep these days. And Ed, I do not believe in Joe Harris's Uncle Remus stories that a rabbit is sharper than a fox. Do you? And then there's the possibility if we did hook up that one could call me an ignoramus meaning that I'm utterly ignorant which I'm not. I know what I want. Also your first name Edward, Ed for short, is easy to remember but it is objectionable.

It's not a name I can picture myself yelling out in a fit of passion. And please note. Ed rhymes with lead that is a potential dangerous element.. Lead acetate is poisonous, lead oxide is explosive. Two characteristics I have noticed in you. And the family name Remus sounds so much like Ramesses who long ago maintained a harem and subsidiary wives who bore him many children.

Your admission that 'you buy condoms by the truckload' indicates that you may be interested in me for something else than my personality. And the phrase 'My mother' has popped up too many times.

Just in case you are interested the mate I chose is handsome, financially successful a caring listener. He dresses with style, appreciates finer things and an imaginative romantic lover. In addition to the above Garth has promised that when he gets older he doesn't have a bald head, able to rearrange furniture, remember to put the toilet seat down, shave on weekends and still breathe.
Sincerely,
Alfa

Ed could not imagine being rejected by Alfa or what it would be like if he placed an ad of his own. To find out he placed one in the *Sun* with the heading: *Single Attractive Realtor Looking for a Mate for Companionship and Possible Marriage.*
There were 33 replies within a week but of these 23 were husbands who wanted to get rid of their wife and the remainder were after all they could get.
Faye for instance wrote that she was spending sleepless nights waiting for a reply. "Seeing your ad makes me think you might be Mr. Right because I like your profession.

You appear to be a builder, a self-made man, striving to make something out of your life. Ed, I'm not after your money but if you have some extra, that's a bonus and our hearts could be in touch for all eternity."

And Christie wrote enclosing a snapshot of her posing by the front gate where a sign read: *Beware of Dog.* The sign and Christie asking for a photograph of his Buick Regal instead of himself was the end of finding a mate by mail. Each reply had a discreet message – they were lonely and could not satisfy Ed's high standards.

Following the negatives Ed was rejuvenated when by a strike of luck he received a creative chain letter from an unknown source who was watching Ed's mate-hunting progress. Unlike most chain letters this one did not cost a penny and read:
"Just bundle up your last interviewee and send her to the man whose name appears at the top of the list. Then add your name to the bottom of the list and send a copy of this letter to five of your friends who are equally having difficulty in finding Mrs. Right.

When your name comes to the top of the list, you will hear from 325 cuties and some are bound to be better suited than those you have dealt with earlier.
Do Not Break This Chain.
Ed we are counting on you.
Signed - A satisfied mate hunter.

Ed listened to the promulgated wisdom of the other mate hunter but did not bundle his last interviewee and send her aloft. He however connected with a youthful Filipina nanny from Cebu City employed by his employer, George Best and his family.

Ed soon found Pasita had six toes on her right foot which in Filipino culture means good luck. Pasita was smart and pretty who ate with bare hands, sometimes with a fork and spoon but never used a knife.

Pasita always wanted to share her food with Ed that included dried fish, rice, odobo, pancit and lechon (roasted piglet) and anything cooked with coconut milk but especially her wanton soup, noodles, spring rolls and deep-fried bananas.

But then Pasita introduced Ed to balu*t* (a boiled fertilized duck egg meant to be an aphrodisiac).

As a non-Pinoy Ed could not imagine having a sexual desire that included crunching on a partially formed baby duck swimming in noxious fluid and one had to eat feathers, beak and claws in order to marry her. One can say that Pasita despite having six toes wasn't lucky because Ed chose not to pursue courting her.

By a fortunate coincidence Ed met up with a First Nations residential school survivor, a lovely lady from the nearby Enoch Cree Reserve named Paulette who was totally different from his pursuits earlier.

Paulette hid herself behind a colorful buckskin jacket and blue sweatpants. She didn't use makeup, had high cheekbones that were rosy and a radiant smile. Her long black hair was left to flow in the wind.

On their second date Paulette said to Ed, "Pray that the casino built on the Enoch Reserve can be a success. Then as soon as I get my government cheque for being an abused child in a White Residential School and I win a Lotto 649 bundle we'll build a cabin in the woods where not a soul

intrudes and you and I as a married couple will tour the world and have a luxurious life in Paradise."
At that point Ed thought he would enjoy Paulette's lifestyle but after several more dates he watched her with suspicion and when the bannock she baked didn't taste like a pizza, Ed left Paulette free.

Edmonton has always been proud of its sports and cultural accomplishments so Ed next hooked up with beautiful Stephanie of Ukrainian heritage after a friend of his, Bohdan, said, "Ed, you are smart, capable, interesting. I have noticed that you have tried the usual activities of finding a 'significant other', including haunting Wal-Mart, Superstore Save On Food and Safeway but I feel you are wasting time. I see where you are still alone and wondering what else you can do, well, I have a suggestion for you."

"I'm listening," Ed said.
"I believe there is someone out there anxious to share the joy of marriage with you."
"And who may she be?"
"My sister Stephanie. I have her photo with me if you care to see it."
After Ed reviewed the photo he found Stephanie self-possessed and did cartwheels like the *Shumka* dancers do at a public concert. Stephanie was well adapted for matrimony with striking qualities any realtor would be glad to have as his wife.
Instantly Ed fell madly in love with Stephanie and each evening they dined at a different restaurant.
It was while they were dining at the top of the Crowne Plaza Hotel where the restaurant at the top kept changing

a view every hour he discovered that Stephanie followed the *Julian* calendar and Ed the *Gregorian*.

That's when Ed apologized and said that he couldn't continue dating Stephanie and when she asked why?

As an *all* professional Ed wiped his forehead and said, "There a difference of 12 days between the two calendars and the difference in culture would confuse me in making appointments and calculating the commission I earn each month."

A day later Ed had a blind date and the Shaw Conference Centre was filled with dancing couples. A large banner hanging from the ceiling read: *Thank You Edmonton for Helping the Destitute & Homeless.*

People in Edmonton agreed the annual charity event was a prime social gathering of the year. The firemen's Annual Ball was second, Capital Ex (formerly Klondike Days) was third and the Fringe Festival fourth.

Ed's towering bubbly blind date, Tara Silver Bell, had more curves than dimples but no regular employment. Tara wore a figure-hugging red sequined cocktail dress gathering appreciate stares from the male patrons as she was nearly seven feet tall and Ed was five-ten..

As Tara and Ed were dancing Ed thought Miss Bell was a ravishing beauty.

They talked about one thing and then another and then Ed said in jest, "Bell, so you must be a ding-dong?"

Tara burst out with laughter, "That's a new one. My previous blind date said I was a dumbbell that was a bit ringy-dingy."

Minutes later Ed and Tara were whirling around the dance floor when Ed said, "The surname Bell was used by Charlotte and Emily Bronte as a pseudonym when they had their novels Jane Eyre and Wuthering Heights published."

Tara expostulated with a smile, "Look," she said, "I'm not into classic literature but I do enjoy Italian pizza."

Tara and Ed danced until 1: 00 a. m. and then went to the Pizza Hut to enjoy what else? – a pizza and a Pepsi. While Ed went to the men's washroom Tara was involved in a spirited conservation with the Pizza Hut manager.

As soon as they finished enjoying their meal Ed walked Tara home under a quiet moonlit sky. Even the owls, crickets and fireflies weren't out that night when Ed asked Tara for another date.

"I can't go out with you?" Tara apologetically replied.

"Is it because of our difference in height?"

"No, it's because while you were in the washroom I found full-time employment making pizzas at Pizza Hut."

The following day as Ed was on his way to take a listing he drove into a parking lot on Whyte Avenue and noticed that a pickup truck with a Saint Bernard dog sitting behind the wheel was rolling towards a pedestrian. The person, Katie, standing there seemed oblivious to the oncoming vehicle, so Ed hit his horn to get her attention. Katie looked up just in time to jump out of the way of the truck's path, and then Ed rushed to Katie's side to see if she was all right.

"I am," Katie assured Ed and continued, "But I hate to think what could have happened to me if that dog hadn't honked."

Ed and Katie began dating but after several days Katie with thoughts flowing in all direction took Ed aside and cautiously said, "Ed to be loved and remain unhappy is interesting but I doubt that I could be your mate."

Katie then handed Ed a list of reasons why it was better for her to choose a dog as a companion rather then a man.

1. Dogs don't necessarily prefer blonds
2. Dogs sometimes dig the garden
3. In a canine world, boxers are sometimes intelligent
4. Dogs will wait patiently outside a clothes shop
5. Dogs can be taught the meaning of NO
6. Dogs can find their way home, even after a really heavy night out
7. A dog is better protection from intruders
8. Puppy love doesn't wear so quickly with a dog
9. A dog will fetch the morning paper for you
10. A dog gets a new coat each winter
11. You can call a dog a schitzu without offending it
12. Dogs do not attack other dogs because of color
13. Dogs are really good with most children
14. Your dog will never refer you as a 'bitch'
15. A dog is less likely to leave a filthy, stinking mess for one to clean up

The following day while riding up in an elevator at the City Centre Mall Ed hooked up with curvaceous Veronica who had a gentle disposition, was financially secure and arguing was a recognized occupation. Ed's object of course was to convince Veronica to be his true love and then while dining in the food court Veronica asked, "Well, much do you love me?" Ed replied, "I love you more than I love my condo mortgage."

It was a wasteful remark drawing Veronica to say, "Ed, my heart knows what the wild goose knows and since I'm a sister of the goose it suggests that I should not be fenced in with a husband if I want my heart at rest. I have fallen in love with nature and hope I haven't disappointed you."

Ed was disappointed as Veronica continued, "You see Ed, the more affection I give to nature and the more she gives me in return."

Ed said that in wooing nature there probably could be less heart-ache and one can admire the landscape, but he would rather prefer to look at Veronica's blue eyes and pretty face with a full moon, a setting sun and the aurora borealis for a background.

With that premise Ed did not pursue Veronica as a possible mate and with a resonant voice said, "Veronica, my love is true but since I have a deadline to meet I will not argue with you."

Veronica lived on a 160 acre farm fronting Muriel Lake near Bonnyville on Highway 28. The farm encompassed a dense forest of pine beetle free pine trees and a gurgling stream. It was a farm where Veronica could observe whether on horseback or foot, frogs in the stream. moss covering rocks turn color from brown to green and hear the robins sing, see the blackbirds build a nest, crows and magpies chasing smaller birds, sparrows on willow trees, hawks soaring the sky, ducks laying eggs, woodpeckers and owls in the forest, loons taking off on the lake like a jet and Canada geese flying either north or south. There use to be many prairie chickens and partridges but like the loon were becoming an extinct specie.

Among the wild animals were: coyotes with an eerie howl at night, rabbits change color each winter from brown to white, groundhogs coming out of hibernation February 2nd, skunks and porcupines crossing her garden path as soon as it got dark, squirrels cracking a nut, chipmunks begging for food to eat from someone's hand and gophers, well, there were too many to count.

Every day sunshine or rain, cold, wet or windy Veronica would explore the flowers: wild roses, dandelions, bluebells and lilies along with fruit bearing saskatoon, chokecherry, pin-cherry and hazel nut bushes.

Veronica also enjoyed watching insects which she said were nature's children: a spider making a web, a bumble bee drawing honey from a blossom and multi colored butterflies flying around and bats in the attic of the old log house. The wasps, black flies and mosquitoes she did not appreciate but nature has its way to balance Planet Earth so she did not attempt to destroy them nor the cutworms, grasshoppers and snails in her vegetable garden. Veronica enjoyed the four seasons but more so summer than winter when it can get bitterly cold and she had the choice of going ice-hole fishing on the lake or read a book in the comfort of the warm fireplace.

Although Veronica had a German shepherd dog to guard the premises and a Persian cat to catch mice she never owned a gun in order to protect herself from the wild animals or if there should be a home invasion by poachers who prey on animals and single women.

Veronica was a determined woman enjoying her undisturbed serenity and nothing, not even Ed whom she liked, would change her mind. Veronica loved nature and to live in solitude more than having a husband for a mate.

CHAPTER 3

Ed was a survivor and in the search for a bride it seemed he experienced more obstacles than King Arthur's knights had in their search for the Holy Grail. Ed was prepared to convert to another faith if that would help to find a suitable mate but was startled to discover that Jews, Muslims and Christians had distinct beliefs about dating. The Jewish method was most methodical, Ed thought, in that Jews turn to their faith communities for helping one to find a date and ultimately wife or a husband.

Islam was out of the question. The Muslim approach for dating was straight forward. It was forbidden. Instead Ed found that Muslims rely on a network of friends who supply suitable mates for their children and above all too-anti Western

Ed found that Christian courtship varied greatly. He next dated Shannon who was an Irish born Catholic but only several times because he learned that the Catholic Church did not believe in divorce and the use of contraceptives.

Ed felt the churches found by Calvin, Dr. Knox and Wesley were to puritanical and following Luther and Ron Hubbard's Scientology did not appeal to him. Ed found problems with Henry V111 as an Anglican Church honcho. With an aroused conscience Ed then studied the Church of the Flying Spaghetti religion and Bertrand Russell's

Celestial Teapot theory about the non- existence of a Supreme Being along with the Church of the Omniscient Google and rejected them too

As Ed still didn't find a mate that suited and the odds seemed against him, he decided to hang out at bars and one evening went for a stroll. As it was getting dark he had not walked further than an unnamed hotel that had an ants' nest of ugly rooms and where customers waited for something exciting to happen.

At the bar Ed met down-and outers, some of them fugitives, gang members and criminals and a dainty sinful kind of a cuss named Tapioca who could be made in a minute. But Tapioca's social life was suddenly destroyed when alcohol brought out the devil in a patron who stabbed her with a hunting knife and more than 50 patrons saw it happen.

At a time when the crime rate in Edmonton was rising Ed did not want to be stabbed by a weirdo wielding a knife or even to be hit across the head with a baseball bat so he brushed off the bar and Tapioca

Ed's next possible mate was Scarlet who he had met at the Sidetrack Café and aside becoming a friend she could do magic. Scarlet entertained friends by performing what Ed thought were slight-of-hand, but it was real magic.

To this point Ed avoided females of questionable character but this time he thought he had hit a jackpot when he and Scarlet fell in love.

Their life was idyllic until Ed's mother phoned and said, "Ed, you are breaking your mother's heart. You haven't visited your parents in a month and now I hear that you are dating a floozy. When was the last time you had your eyes examined?"

"I'm sorry Mom. But I've been busy listing and selling real estate, doing charity work for Meals on Wheels and dating Scarlet. I assure you Scarlet is no floozy and I want you to meet her."

Although Scarlet dreaded the moment she agreed to meet Ed's parents and when she did for dinner, his father said, "Never in my entire life would I have thought that Ed would have hooked up with such a beauty."
And his mother said shaking Scarlet's hand, "Oh, you poor dear," and then hugged her.
Ed's father then signaled that Ed say grace.
"OK father," Ed replied and after bowing his head said:
"Dear God
Ruba dub, dub
Thank you for the grub.
Some have hunger, but no meat
Some have meat, but can not eat
Bless those who are able
To enjoy the food on this table
Forgive us sinners
And pray that Scarlet and I become winners
Lord we give you thanks and praise
Bless Scarlet and me throughout the coming days."

During the dinner, things went well. Among Scarlet's assets besides doing magic, she was an excellent conversationalist and had a sense of humor.
After dinner Ed's mother took him aside and said, "I apologize. Scarlet seems like an ideal mate for you. You must make an effort to marry her."
True to his word Ed proposed next night and Scarlet agreed to marry him.

Of course, Ed's mother insisted that the couple have a grandiose June wedding at the No Name Universal Church and a reception at the Westin Hotel. She met Scarlet many times to plan the June wedding.

Ed's mother picked out Scarlet's wedding gown, her bridesmaids and their gowns, rented the ballroom for the reception, hired a band, ordered flowers, made out invitations and did everything that needed to be done to make the wedding perfect.

Scarlet merely had to nod her agreement with Ed's mother choices. Ed rented a tux and hired a limousine. His best man planned a bachelor party at a strip club.

The night before the wedding Scarlet came to Ed worried. "You know Ed," she said, "I have never been inside a church before. I don't know how to behave."

Ed placed an arm around her. "Don't worry. Simply walk slowly up the aisle. When you reach Reverend Taylor, just follow my lead. Do what I do or what Reverend Taylor tells you. There's nothing to worry about."

Finally the great day came. First Ed and the best man arrived and took their places by the altar. Ed was dressed in his tuxedo and appeared utterly irresistible. His dark hair was slightly ruffled and his eyes full of adoration as he looked towards his bride to be.

The church was filled with Ed and Scarlet relatives, friends and neighbors.

The bride and her entourage arrived carrying a bouquet of miniature white roses. As the organist played *The Wedding March* the flower girl sprinkled petals as Scarlet made her way up the aisle.

Next came the ring bearer followed by the bridesmaids. In her white gown, her coiffured hair partially covered by her veil, Scarlet solemnly walked up the aisle.

Ed's marriage was within his grasp. It inevitably was yanked however, when something unusual happened at the No Name Universal Church as Scarlet passed the last pew. There was a rumbling sound inside like that of an earthquake. Next Scarlet's white dress turned black. Smoke curled out of Scarlet's ears. Before Scarlet reached the altar she burst into flames and disappeared in a horrendous cloud of sulfurous smoke.

That's when a thunderous evil voice called out, "Hold it, Ed! Back off! Let's not get carried away! She's mine! You shall not have Scarlet!"

Everyone in the church started screaming and running about. The scene turned to chaos.

No one was more stunned than Ed. His lady love had disappeared.

Following three days of grieving Ed wondered if it was possible to love someone more than once. That thought disappeared when he visited City Hall to pay his annual property taxes where he met Kelly who was chain-smoking during her break. Kelly also kept a day-timer on her desk and between smoking and drinking coffee did Tai Chi. At first glance Ed thought Kelly was a possible mate. As it turned out however, Kelly was considerably older and a member of the City Council which was considering initiating a host of bylaw fines, including the use of a radar camera to catch traffic violators. Ed was against the use of a radar gun in order to increase city coffers and wondered instead of levying fines why city streets filled with hundreds of potholes weren't repaired. Ed therefore disassociated himself with Kelly.

The Purple Onion is a favorite hangout in Edmonton. Next to its long bar is a juke box. A pool table is located to one side of it. Towards the back there are tables and a dance area. Most weekends regulars come for their pick-me up. On Friday and Saturday nights, a local band plays there. On these nights the place as a rule is mobbed.

The smoke was so thick, one could cut it with a knife and the volume of noise made conversation a shouting match.

It was on such a Friday evening that Ed sat at the bar when a most knockout gorgeous woman he had ever seen sat on a stool next to him. Her low cocktail dress revealed so deep it was like staring into a bottomless pit. Her waist was narrow, her hip flaring.

Her ivory sculptured face was capped by flaming blond hair, her full lips were devilish carmine and the mascara on her green catlike eyes seemed to make them glow mysteriously.

Eying her carefully Ed was about to ask Britney for a date believing she was his dream mate. He lost Brittney however, as soon as her husband cop sat next to her.

Hearing that Ed was having a difficult time in finding a mate his father said, "Ed, all relationships are a balance of power. Eventually you may find a one.

Why don't you try Toastmasters or attend an Arts Festival and Sushi bars is a great place to meet females."

Although Ed had no fear of public speaking he enjoyed dinning in restaurants more so the following evening he darted across the street from his office to *Deep Sushi* where inside the smells of cologne and soy sauce permeated the environment.

The lights were low and single women seemed plenty. In the end however, Ed was piqued not because of the raw fish on the menu or that there was a *No Smoking* sign posted, but because Dahlia whom he met, was low in smarts and knew nothing about the Arts. The sole experience of having a meal with her was based on whether or not one got a hormonal high. Neither did.

Always on the go, the following night Ed was out with Lina who was a full-time actress at the Citadel Theatre and could double as a tree. Lina who was tall and graceful owned four pet mice which she had taught to sing. Ed accompanied Lina as she took the rodents to a Talent Agency in downtown Edmonton believing she could make a fortune promoting them instead of acting.

Lina placed a suitcase on the agent's desk, opened it and in seconds the Field Mouse Quartet was positioned on the table. With the snap of Lina's finger the mice began singing like the Beatles. She snapped her finger again and this time the four mice sang an aria from Die Fledermaus. Lina snapped her finger a third time and the mice sang a medley of Johnny Cash tunes.

"Well," Lina said to Ed and then to the agent, "What do you think?"

"Can't use them," the agent replied.

"What do you mean, you can't use them? What's the matter with the act?"

"To tell you the truth," the agent said, "The mice don't sing that badly but the leader looks quite a bit like yourself."

"What to you mean?"

"He needs a face lift."

Disappointed with the outcome of the interview Lina
let the mice loose and it was several months later that
Edmonton had the greatest mice attack in its history. The
infestation was so great that the local SPCA got rid of 100
cats in a single day. But wait!
The original Field Mice Quartet was clever and survived.
Lina then took the mice to a karaoke party at the Cook
County Saloon where they sang a medley of Country and
Western songs and won first prize.
A talent scout was watching them sing and invited Lina
and the mice to record an album in Nashville. Any
romantic inclination that Ed may have had with Lina
discontinued.

But another was about to begin when two days later at a
time when news got uglier and uglier - more wars, more
crime, more terrorism, more famine and more pollution.
At this point Ed entered the Midnight Sun golf tournament
in boomtown Fort McMurray 250 miles north east of
Edmonton on the dangerous Highway 63.where many
travelers have motor vehicle accidents and are killed.
The Fort Mac region is home the world's largest reservoir
of crude bitumen and the largest of three major oil sands
deposits in Alberta, along with nearby Peace River and
Cold Lake deposits.

On the first day of arrival Ed was attracted to his golfing
partner, a lovely young fascinating woman, a perverse
Madonna by the name of Becky, a stenographer at Suncor,
a bitumen oil company.
Ed and Becky discovered that during midnight on June
21 the sun had no intention of setting and golfers from
throughout the world fought their way through swarms of
black flies and mosquitoes. After the tournament began it

was on stop number 3, and a difficult par 4 with a water trap next to a tree, Becky teed-off and her ball landed into the water where the ball began to sink. As it was sinking a fish grabbed the ball into its mouth. At that very moment a raven (there are many in the north) plucked the ball out of the water and began carrying it aloft. As the raven soared higher and higher believing the ball would eventually hatch, a bolt of thunder startled the bird which dropped the fish onto a boulder and after several bounces the ball rolled right into the hole and Becky had a hole in one.

"Congratulations," Ed said and gave Becky a hug.

"Now see if you can get a hole in one. I bet you a Canada goose feather that you can't,"

Becky said and thought why she scratched less than Ed was because she was on a fat-free diet.

Becky continued, "And it's not because of the Seven-Year Itch that you are scratching more often than I do."

Ed accepted the challenge and it was on hole # 6, a par 3, that Ed placed the ball on the T and said "I do not believe in the current airy-fairy stuff that your toenails should be painted green."

Ed closed his eyes and swung with all his might and the ball ricochet off several boulders and took a fantastic bounce onto the green and into the cup for a hole in one.

Becky congratulated Ed and said, "Now we each have a hole in one. Let's try for another."

"Just for fun," Ed said

Although Ed had a hole in one he would desperately try to get another but because the flies and mosquitoes were after him and he didn't use an insect repellant, he scratched, flubbed and didn't do well.

When it was Becky's turn her ball soared into the air where on the fairway a raven caught it while flying in the direction of the green. The ball however slipped out of the raven's beak and dropped into the pouch of a squirrel. Believing the ball as an oversized nut the squirrel ran to the flag and popped the ball into the hole for safe-keeping without ever touching the ground.

"I did it! I did it! Two holes in one on the same course. I can't believe it!" Becky exclaimed.

Neither could Ed but both holes-in-one were witnessed by tournament officials who after searching the latest edition of a *Golf Fact Book* an official said, "The approximate chance of someone shooting two holes in one on the same golf course like Becky did, is 727 million and occur once in 2, 741 years."

Although Ed was delighted that Becky had won the tournament he wasn't impressed with the risks oil producers in the region were taking towards the environment and the prevention of ducks getting stuck in settling ponds. These tar sands lie in the sparsely populated forest and muskeg and contain 1.7 trillion barrels of bitumen.

Speaking to Becky following the tournament Ed said, "Look, in ratifying the Kyoto Protocol, Canada agreed to reduce, by 2012, its greenhouse emissions by 6% with respect to 1990 but since then greenhouse emissions have increased by 24% and the Fort McMurry area Oil Sands production has increased, 4.4 percent of Canada's total green house emissions. The Fort McMurray region is world's largest emitter of greenhouse gases. There are risks posed by large scale mining operations, causing damage to the natural environment."

Becky's response was, "Objections to the Oil Sands project have been clouded by advocates like you and Green Peace and the Sierra Club. Most of the oil now can be produced using the most recent developed in-sity technology and your assessment of the oil industry in Alberta doesn't hold water."

"First, I do not now what *in-sity* means and speaking of water just take a look at the local lakes, ponds and rivers that are polluted destroying the habitat of the birds and animals.

Also consider the health of the local aboriginal people. And if nothing is done about the current critical infrastructure, shortage of accommodations, high rent, schools, hospital and Highway 63 based on the last five years your and my family will experience a most devastating financial crises since the Great Depression in the thirties."

Since Ed and Becky had different thoughts about the Oil Sands projects, estimated at over $15-billion, and to the environment and the climate changes, Ed did not consider Becky, although intelligent, as a possible mate but still they remained friends.

By July 1st Ed, who could easily make friends, was dating Kate from Washington D. C. who was visiting her brother in Edmonton. It was a statutory commemoration of Canada's 1867 birthday when Kate curiously asked, "Ed, does Canada have a July 4th?"

"It' does but it falls on July 1st which is today," Ed replied and continued, "For the Chinese Canadians it is known as Humiliation *Day* and too many other Canadians as Moving Day and some just relax and drink beer."

Ed and Kate were watching the night fireworks that started fireworks of their own when Kate asked, "Ed, how do you feel about the seal hunt off the coast of Newfoundland each spring? I think it's sickening."

"Despite what Bridget Bardot and Paul McCartney have to say I'm in favor of the hunt. To get the record straight there are less seals killed than innocent Iraq people due to the American invasion of that country.

It's less brutal than cock fighting which is a national sport in Puerto Rico which is an American protectorate. And do you want to know something else?"

"What?"

"Although President Bush says he has a personal relationship with Jesus there's underground dog and cockfighting fighting in America where people derive pleasure and enjoyment. So before you talk about the seal hunt on the east coast of Canada you better find out what your own country is doing that is brutal and do you want to know something else?"

"What?"

'The Iraq war and the one in Afghanistan will eventually bankrupt America."

Ed and Kate, who voted Republican, did not agree on many subjects including Canadians having a passport-like document in order to enter America and Health Care. There while watching the Canada Day fire works their dating diplomatically ended. Ed withdrew from Kate but not the world of dating.

Also during the month of July Ed attended the Capital EX (formerly Klondike Days) which featured an international market place with exhibition booths, a midway carnival rides, crafts, horse racing and fireworks. The exhibition also featured some of the best known international entertainers and bands. Over 800,000 people took in the ten-day July event.

It was at Capital EX that Best Realty had a booth and while manning it Ed met Dinah from Winnipeg who was a striking beauty with a sultry voice.

Ed and Dinah initially enjoyed each other's company that evening until Dinah exuded her confidence and she said that Winnipeg's Red River Exhibition was a better attraction than Capital EX and the Bombers were a better CFL football team than the Eskimos he became disappointed.
After Dinah said that she could uncover the Da Vinci code inside the Manitoba Legislative buildings Ed felt her I. Q. was lowering and suddenly he lost interest in her.

Ed's next move was to attend the annual August Heritage Days Festival in Hawreluck Park where more than 70 different ethnicities participate each August featuring a variety of ethnic food, song and dance.
It was at the festival that Ed met lovely Angelina of Italian heritage.
Although Ed enjoyed Italian home-made wine, spaghetti and pizza he felt he could not promise that he could grow beans attached to six-foot poles or preserve Italian cultural and religious traditions should they get married.

Next Ed was having a super-time with Rizza who was a participant at the Fringe Festival that is the second largest in the world. Scotland has the largest Fringe. Rizza wore the current rage D&G sun glasses that covered her entire face that seemed to have had a facial botched plastic surgery. It was while Ed and Rizza were in conversation that Ed was suddenly called by his office to list a farm near Sherwood Park.

Since time was of the essence Ed had to depart suddenly without having time to ask the charming lady for a date and by the time he returned Ed had lost her to another mate-searcher.

The following weekend the Edmonton Chamber of Commerce held its annual August Scavenger Hunt promoting tourism.

The challenge was to visit downtown locations while deciphering clues, solving puzzles and answering local and provincial trivia questions.

Ed coupled up with Sarah, a visitor from Alaska. The couple drove to Canada Place, Francis Winspear Centre, Stan Milner Library, Citadel Theatre and Alberta Art Gallery.

This was followed with a visit to City Hall, Muttart Conservatory, Northlands Park, Telus World of Science Centre, Legislature Buildings and the Provincial Museum where Sarah said to a guard while holding a list, "Sir, Ed and I are on a scavenger hunt, and all we still need is three grains of wheat, a pork chop and a piece of used carbon paper in order to win a prize."

"Wow!" the museum security guard said, "Who sent you on such a challenging hunt?"

"The Edmonton Chamber of Commerce."

Although Ed and Sarah did not win a prize Sarah left him a *Girlfriend's Lament* before she left town. It read:

It was the day of the Scavenger hunt when I was in your kitchen;

I was cooking and baking and moaning and bitchin'.

I've been in your condo for hours and did not stop to rest.

Ed, your bedroom is a disaster, just look at the mess.

Take a look at all the people we had to feed.
You expected all the trimmings but not what I need!
My feet are blistered. I've got cramps in my legs.
I was so nervous that I spilled a bowl full of eggs.
Oops, there's a knock on your condo door and the telephone is ringing.
At the same time the microwave oven is dinging.
Two pies in the oven, desert almost done,
Your duct taped cookbook is soiled and not the right one.
Ed, I have all I can stand. I can't be your mate any more,
In walks your condo neighbor, John who spills his liquor on the floor.
He weaves and he wobbles, his balance is unsteady;
Then he grins as he chuckles, "Sarah, is the eggnog ready?"
John looks around and with total regret,
And asks, "Sarah aren't you through with Ed yet?"
As quick as a flash I reach for the kitchen knife;
He loses an earlobe although I wanted his life!
John flees from your condo in terror and pain.
"My God Woman!" he screams. "Sarah you're going insane!"
Now what was I doing, and what is that smell?
It's the pies! They're burned all to hell!
I hate to admit it Ed, when I make a mistake,
But I put them in the oven on Broil instead of Bake.
Are there still more Edmonton discomforts ahead?
Ed, this isn't my life style, I'd rather be dead.
Don't get me wrong. I love Edmonton.
And the scavenger hunt was lot of fun.
But I promise you one thing, if I live till next year,
You won't find me pulling my hair out here.

It was Sarah's turn to say, "Best of luck in your mate hunting."

The following weekend Ed entered a three-day September Riverside Golf Course Singles Only Tournament where in each foursome there were two men and two women. On the first day Ed was paired up with Amanda who he thought he would like to date so he casually said to her, "Do you believe marriage is like a lottery?"
As soon as Amanda replied, "No, in a lottery a woman has a chance."
That did it. Ed did not ask Amanda for a date.

Ed didn't take no for and answer and during the second day of the tournament was paired off with a foursome that included Jade who he thought would make an ideal mate. After they reached the 13th hole Jade's ball landed in a sand trap where after several tries to get it on the fairway she picked up her golf club and broke it into two.

Jade then picked up her golf bag, tore it into shreds and finally the golf balls she had left flung them into the woods. Ed could not cope with temperamental females so he did not ask Jade for a date.
On the third day Ed was paired off with Brandy who was three years older than Jade and still paying off her students' loan and failing to return 50 books to the library. On the 9th hole however, Ed and Brandy got into an argument over the definition of the words *hooker* and *tricks* and neither would give way.
Ed decided if he was going to be the bread winner, any possible romantic relationship should end, there in the middle of the golf course.

As taking part in a Singles Only golf tournament did not work Ed decided to have his hairstyle changed. Not anything dramatic, just a tinge above his natural color somewhere between brown and black and streaked in the middle.

But that didn't work nor the use of a different underarm deodorant, red socks instead of black, a strict fat-free diet, exercising, wearing dark colored glasses or growing a mustache that is when his mother suggested, "Ed, try riding the local transit."

Ed always took his mother seriously. To make sure his search did not lose momentum Ed climbed into a bus at the bottom of Bellamy Hill hoping a lovely lady would sit by him.

That did not happen however, because when a gargantuan male sat next to him climbing the hill was impossible, not the fault of neither the passenger nor that his wife was the driver, but the bus unexpectedly stopped. Due to its age the vehicle had to be towed to the city transportation garage for a major repair.

After having a bad weekend Ed walked into a tattoo parlor and enquired about the possibility of having one, not a parlor but an ink injection.

"Women love men with their tattoo on their arm, that's why so many jailbirds get one," the tattooist said but after Ed was explained the process he felt having a heart tattooed on his chest was to painful and one could cause an infection.

Feeling hungry Ed asked the tattooist where he could find packaged dates to enjoy. The tattooist looked rather oddly and said, "You can try the Yellow Pages under the heading *Escorts.* Ed wasn't interested in an escort showing up in his condo and that evening his mother called again and said, "Ed, why don't you spend some time at the Riverside Healthcare Resort where unattached females hang out?"

"That's an excellent idea," Ed said and during the weekend had a conversation with Candy who was from Newfoundland.

While sitting at a spa table Ed asked the stout lady, "What is the main diet of Newfoundlanders?"

"Fish," Candy said.

"I always thought fish was a brain food but do you want to something?"

"What?"

"I'll be candid. To me you appear to be the most unintelligent woman I have ever met."

"Is that so? Well can you imagine what I would look like if fish wasn't part of my diet?"

"You'd look like Godzilla," Ed replied and that was the end of any relationship with Candy.

Ed did not succeed with Candy or with a pretty French-speaking la crème de la crème of a lady from Quebec. During a preliminary vis-à-vis conversation Mademoiselle Fifi said, "I have traveled throughout the world by car, ship, train and plane.

"I've been to Paris, Rome, Warsaw, London and Tokyo and know all there is to know about perfume, fashion trends, fog, amber and sushi."

"Ooh! la! la! I find that interesting," Ed said. "You appear to be a hot potato but do you mind if I ask a personal question?"

"Go ahead."

"Are you bilingual?"

"Oui."

"Now tell me, how do feel about Quebec's sovereignty and the province separating from the rest of Canada?"

"Mon Dieu," I'm in favor," Fifi replied but Ed wasn't so he asked Fifi to do what happened to the Titanic years ago – split, and Ed's search for a mate continued.

At this point Ed's search for a mate and happiness was in a mess. He had not convinced a female to be his lifetime mate, only to find out that day by day it got worse and friends of his constantly reminded him, "Do not let your mother down."

In order to speed up his search Ed took a three-day 101 evening course at Grant MacEwan College on *Dating and Food* which mainly dealt on how to reach one's heart through the food they ate'.

At the college Ed met three stunning wanabe females who wanted to find a mate for themselves but unfortunately neither cooked for a male before. The first was Claire. Claire and Ed agreed to a guest- relationship where she would visit his condo on weekends to do his laundry and prepare his meals but there wouldn't be any sex.

Claire was an excellent cook and made the best ice cubes one ever tasted. Her specialty was fried water but one weekend while having breakfast she got fancy with her cooking and screwed up the cornflakes.

To Claire a balanced meal was one which Ed had a 50-50 chance of surviving. She sliced tomatoes by throwing them through the screen door and one day she had turkey on the menu and Ed was tickled. Claire had forgotten to take off the feathers. Things between Clair and Ed came to a head however, when Ed discovered a crate containing

12 dozen eggs which were left near the kitchen oven and chicks began hatching.

Seeing the chicks pop up one after another Ed said, "Claire, why don't you do something? Say something interesting to the chicks?"

Claire got on top of the crate and screamed, "Chickens of the world unite for better egg laying conditions!"

That's when the relationship with Clair ended and a new one began with Alice 'Big' Rock, who he also met while taking the dating-food course at the college.

The relationship with Alice 'Big' Rock didn't last long however, because she fell over one of her meatballs and injured her spleen.

Ed called 911 and an ambulance took this possible mate to Emergency at the Misercoridia Community Hospital and when she felt better was transferred home to Lethbridge where she lay in the sun on the Waterton Lake beach.

Alice 'Big' Rock lay in the sun often, the heat that month was so intense that she became petrified and spent the rest of her life in isolation

Why was this cook so afflicted? Because according to geologists she was deposited on Planet Earth during the Ice Age.

Ed did not believe that theory however, but one suggested by Chief Flying Eagle of the nearby Blood Indian Reserve who said that why Alice 'Big' Rock was so afflicted this way was because she had stolen a blanket at the Waterton Hotel where she was previously employed.

Today Alice 'Big' Rock is an imposing sight and site in southern Alberta where tourists see her image near Fort McLeod where Highways 2 and 3 converge. Today Alice 'Big' Rock is a tourist landmark attraction for the entire world to see.

Ed's next weekend relationship was with Janna but on a Friday evening when she began her weekend relationship Ed found Janna depressed so he asked, "What's the matter? "Your cooking and baking are excellent."

"Well, to be truthful," Janna said, "Some of the people I work with are spreading lies that before I met you I had twins."

"Relax," Ed said, "I make it a rule to believe only one-half of what I hear."

Actually Janna was an excellent cook. "Your blueberry pies are delicious," Ed said.

"Thank you."

"And the half-moon decorations on the crust, how did you make them?"

Ed was surprised when Janna answered, "By using my false teeth."

Janna was known throughout Edmonton as an exceptionally creative cook. For example she wrapped spaghetti around meat balls and called them, "Hot yoyos."

She could cook up an order of fish in ten minutes: fish steak, fish croquettes and fish salad. Once a year those who ate her fish meals got the urge to jump into the North Saskatchewan River and spawn.

Since Ed couldn't swim he let Janna loose and thus his weekend relationships with the three lovely Edmonton lady cooks ended. But another began when Ed was taking photos of the downtown Edmonton tall buildings and at the Churchill Square met Lucille.

After several dates however, Ed discovered that Lucille converted from the Satanist to the Lucifiarian cult which enabled her to have her predictictons come true. She predicted that the real estate market would soon crash and the interesting part was that Shirley had already won a furnished luxury home in the Riverbend subdivision during the Caritas Hospital raffle, a motorcycle, an organ, and a trip to Auschwitz.

The real clincher came when Shirley predicted Lotto 649 numbers and actually won two lotteries in a row becoming wealthy. Not as wealthy as Warren Buffet or Bill Gates but still got mentioned in the *Financial Post* thus abandoning Ed to live in Switzerland.

Because of a real estate transaction Ed didn't search for mate the next two days but on the third returned to Churchill Square to take more pictures of tall buildings that might be repossessed or for sale and met Cassandra where they became fast friends. Ed thought Cassandra was the best thing since sliced bread was invented.

She was no troll under the High Level Bridge but had one trait that Ed did not appreciate – she had a perpetual smile on her face and was a daughter of a witch.

Ed and Cassandra however, updated each other on their lives – the sales Ed had made and Cassandra her involvement with Unidentified Flying Objects.

The following afternoon an unidentified triangular-shaped UFO with rows of bright orange colored lights flashing, landed in the Churchill Square, abducted Cassandra and left just as fast as it had landed.

Ed described the three alien creatures in the UFO as humanoid and 3 to 4 feet tall. They had dark brown, hairless skin, big triangular heads with three short 'horns' on top, and huge red eyes that were vertically oval.

According to Ed the most extraordinary encounter was witnessed by security guards at the Edmonton Centre and wondered why the Canadian government hadn't started a special investigation to make certain that they weren't terrorists and no nuclear weapons were inside the object. And further more since there's a UFO launching pad in Saint Paul, a town in east central Alberta, why did one land in Edmonton?

Meanwhile a science and technology professor at the University of Alberta, when he heard about the UFO landing said, "The evidence that Planet Earth is being visited by extraterrestrial civilization is now extensive both in scope and detail. In totality, it comprises a body of evidence which at the very least supports the general assessment that extraterrestrial life has been detected in Edmonton, and that a vigorous program of research and serious diplomatic initiative is warranted."

Once thought the preserve of cranks, weirdo's and eccentrics this Edmonton UFO phenomenon soon caught the attention not only of mainstream University of Alberta academia but also Alberta's leading ufologist, Minerva, who was a good candidate to become Ed's bride. While driving down a hill they came upon a perfect crop circle in a wheat field along the Queen E 2 highway near the International Airport.

To Ed and Minerva the sound of music being linked to crop circles was most intriguing and Minerva wanted to do research.

Ed parked his Buick Regal and as soon as the couple entered the circle to encode the design, a magic-like thing happened – there was an electric charge which stopped their wrist watches from ticking.

The crop circle, 30 meters in diameter and the City of Calgary logo inside, was an artistic accomplishment to say the least.

Ed remained open-minded that it may have been created by aliens from another planet. He was skeptical at Minerva's theory that during the night the Calgary Tourist Bureau created the circle to spite the city of Edmonton and garner more tourists for itself.

Ed's dating Minerva was cut short after she said, "Ed, I don't take anything at face value, either when presented by academics or the ill-informed media. The crop circle phenomenon has inspired me to the point that I want to take time off chasing unidentified flying objects in order to do my own crop circle investigation."

While renewing his library card at the Stanley Milner Public Library Ed met Grace who he found intelligent and fascinating but naïve. Grace, who was single, had just published a sensational novel *Edmonton Place* featuring sex, violence, hypocrisy, decadence, corruption and scandals in Edmonton and making the *Edmonton Journal* Best Seller List.

Grace had completed her novel based on what she had seen in every day Edmonton and centered on the fortune of two single- parent women.

Grace described the city of nearly one-million as a petty, a mean spirited town with the oil, natural gas, ice sculpturing and agricultural industries booming in which rape, alcoholism, drugs, stabbings, racial gangs, aggressive panhandling, mental illness, home invasion and sexual passion seethe behind a façade of old-fashioned propriety.

In a conversation with Ed, Grace said that she had experienced hostility during book signings and on talk shows although the function of her novel wasn't to educate but to entertain. Censors' however, thought differently. The scandalous novel was banned in several cities declaring it was *indecent* and the Alberta Parent Teacher Association as *a complete debasement of taste.*

A sign in front of the Calgary Library read: "This Library does not carry the novel entitled *Edmonton Place*. If you want it go to Edmonton."

The Edmonton Library did stock her novel but there were no plaques or statues to be found in Grace's honor.

Edmonton Place may have seemed like a new and alien world but in some ways it was as old as the Province of Alberta born in 1905. Ed thought the novel was trash, but that didn't exclude his interest in the subject matter. Still he did not want to start a relationship with Grace but thought he would write a book of his own as soon as he got married.

Shortly after Ed read the novel *Edmonton Place* he met Iris while waiting to see Dr. Hardy at the Medical Clinic on Jasper Avenue. The Alberta government had just laid out a frame work for two-tiered health care.

Under the plan to reshape Medicare patients would have the option of paying for some non-emergency procedures, such as knee, cataract and hip surgeries.

The health care reforms would also allow doctors to practice in both public and private health care systems. Iris agreed with the change but Ed didn't and there at the medical centre was a disagreement.

Iris believed the proposed reforms would reduce the cost of spiraling health care.

"These will be alternatives for people that can afford to pay for them," she said.

Ed, a Friend of Medicare, was critical about the repercussions for the public system and pointed out to Iris, in no uncertain terms by countering Iris and his critics by saying, "The proposed plan allowing surgeon to work in both public and private systems will pull doctors out of the public system and waiting lists will become longer. And what doctor would then want to practice in a rural community? Its way of saying the two-tiered health proposal is one for the rich and another for the poor.

It's important in any reform of the health care that the public system be protected. Why doesn't the government do something by making the waiting period shorter and then there will be no need for a private system."

Although Ed thought Iris had potential to be a mate he did not pursue the matter.

Ed then met Jane who was plain and appeared in pain. The good-looking nurse was employed by the Capital Health public relations department. Capital Health had just past an ordinance that Canada geese living in the region, particularly in Edmonton, had worn out their welcome.

After the second date as a member of the *Coalition to Prevent Destructions of Urban Canada Geese*, Ed asked Jane, "But why the ordinance?"

"Because urban geese peck up lawns and golf courses, and in the process cover them with blobs of doo-doo which is a health hazard."

Jane said that the City of Edmonton officially tried scaring the Canada geese by chasing them in golf carts, and by blasting a starter gun placed at strategic locations and, "City Council was going to recommend to local restaurants to include cooked geese 'specials' on their menu."

The Mayor's exasperation was echoed by many who lived in Edmonton so Capital Health sent out a bulletin recommending the following ways for the public to reduce the number of Canada geese in the city.

1. Shaking goose eggs or coating them with vegetable oil so eggs don't hatch.
2. Rounding up the adult geese and shipping them to Calgary.
3. Using inflatable plastic coyotes and dead geese decoys, especially on the North Saskatchewan River and nearby wheat fields.
4. Use swans, imported from Grande Prairie, an even bigger bully that kicks out the geese.
5. Giving the male geese vasectomies.
    Although Ed did not manage to date Michelle because she was already engaged to someone else he learned from her that:
6. Canada geese relieve themselves more often than animals, every three minutes, if they eat only grass.
7. The life span is 8 to 10 years but some geese have been known to live into their thirties.
8. While Canada geese are refuted to have a mate for a lifetime, some geese do divorce and make planes crash.
9. Canada geese do not lay eggs until they are several years old. After that they lay an average of five or six a year and when grown up can cause planes to crash.
10. In Rockland, New York Canada geese are such a problem the town's health commissioner says he would like to kill 8,000 of them.

It was a week later that Ed hooked up with Roxana but only for a short while. After several dates Ed discovered that the lovely lady was a militant ecological activist of the Save the Forest protesters. And the following day, instead of dating Ed, led a demonstration at Rundle Park to wipe out toilet paper. The group was demanding a complete world-wide ban on the use of toilet paper. An angry throng of about 50 nature lovers vehemently rallied against the human slaughter of millions upon millions of beautiful, pure innocent trees annually used to make the ubiquitous tissue rolls. The irate throng then stunned curious onlookers by collectively dropping their pants and defecating en mass on the lush green lawn. They then proceeded to wipe themselves with whatever Mother Nature had kindly provided near by with fallen leaves, moss, pine cones, bird feathers, dead squirrel tails and even coattails of passed out winos.

After finalizing a real estate deal Ed was heading home late one afternoon, and driving above the prescribed speed limit on the Yellowhead Highway. Ed looked at the rear view mirror and noticed a police cruiser with red flashing lights following him.

"I think I can outgun this cop," Ed thought so he floored it.

Both cars were racing down the highway, 80, 90, 100 miles per hour. Finally as his speedometer reached 110 Ed gave up and pulled his Buick Regal to the curb.

At that point the police officer got out of the cruiser and approached Ed.

The officer leaned down and said to Ed, "Listen Mister, I have had a lousy day, and I just want to go home. Give me the excuse and I'll let you go."

Ed thought for a moment and replied, "Two weeks ago my potential girl friend ran off with a cop and I thought you were trying to give her back to me."

The following evening Ed picked a copy of the *Washington Post* newspaper and then while relaxing in his condo read Romantic Poems the paper published while holding a competition with the most romantic first line, but the least romantic, second. Ed felt the poems were a reflection on his search for an ever-loving mate and read:

> Love may be beautiful, love may be bliss.
> But I only slept with you because I was pissed.

I thought I could love no other	I love your smile, face and your eyes
Until, that is, I met your brother	Darn it, I'm good at telling lies.
Of loving beauty you float with grace.	My darling, my beautiful possible wife;
If only you could hide your face.	Marrying you would screw up my life.
Kind, intelligent, loving and hot.	I see your face when I'm dreaming.
This describes everything you are not.	That's why I always wake up screaming.
I want to feel your sweet embrace,	What inspired this amorous rhyme?
But don't take that paper bag of your face.	Two parts vodka, one part lime

CHAPTER 4

By now Ed's world of finding a suitable mate was crumbling. His good looks, charm and an absolute refusal to conform to the society around him would not stop him. Ed now was determined more than ever and would stop at nothing in his quest to find a suitable mate, excluding murder of course. This young man when he attended the Edmonton Opera production of Mozart's *Don Giovanni* met the leading, bubbly witty, lovely lady, Samantha, he met his match. As Ed wanted to be a successful realtor, Samantha equally wanted to eventually be a leading operatic star at the Met in New York or Milan's jewel, La Scala. As one must plow before he/she harvests Ed and Samantha's dating process did not continue after several dinners at the *Red Lobster Restaurant* because marriage was not on Samantha's agenda.

Ed's search for a bride was daunting and since his deadline was fast approaching he kept searching and the following week when the annual October Rodeo and Jamboree took place and cowboy mating was prevalent; Ed thought he was in the driver's seat.

He shed his business suit and got dressed in a cowboy outfit, which was made of blue denim, a white cowboy hat, a black belt with a big buckle and black leather boots.

Since Ed's latest dates were a disaster he thought, "This time I'm going to lasso me a mate tonight," and waited in line outside Rexall Place where the rodeo was held.

It is said that a strange phenomenon occurs during October Rodeo Week. It is more than a week of riding horses, bulls, calves and chuck wagon races. It's also a week of dancing, fiddling and socializing.

It's also mating season for some counterfeit folks who two-step from bar to bar under the guise of Western wear and the square dancer becomes an icon of a certain kind of image.

It's a mistype that represents machismo and freedom and Ed for his part was ready for the attack.

Once inside Rexall Place Ed met Dusty who was upbeat, positive and in a playful mood. The evening began with Ed and Dusty doing a two-step, a foxtrot, a round and a polka where on several occasions Dusty got dropped to the floor after being spun around and around, colliding with other couples.

In between dances, like other prospects, Dusty had her love story. Her boyfriend had been killed at the Calgary Stampede when he fell off a raging bull. And as time pressed on Dusty got pie-eyed and wanted to drink Ed under the table.

It was after midnight that Ed finally said, "Dusty you are either flaky or careless, maybe both. Although I love dancing, a lifetime with you isn't my idea of being compatible. And do you want to know something else?"

"What?"

"I'll have to see a chiropractor in the morning to put my back in order."

The following morning while a chiropractor was examining Ed's back and at the same time listening to Supper news and sports CHED radio, Ed was surprised when the station management phoned him and announced that in a recent survey the station had taken Ed was voted the most popular bachelor in Edmonton.

The station also offered Ed a prize to take part in a Love-At-First-Sight charity contest. Ed and a chosen mate were given an opportunity for an all-expense paid honeymoon trip with free golfing for a week to Vancouver. The single female contestants between 18 and 30 were screened by the station staff until there were only three finalists left that Ed did not know, and had the privilege of interviewing each with the possibility of one becoming his bride.

It was love-at-first sight event and after Ed's photo appeared in the *Sun* newspaper hundreds single female candidates from all walks of life and as far as Red Deer and Grande Prairie, each seeking happiness, paid $20 and hollered, "Pick me! Pick me for the opportunity of becoming Ed's bride!"

Of the three finalists Ed first interviewed Rita but she wasn't as pretty as Bonita and Bonita wasn't as pretty as Margarita Anne who was gorgeous and whose surname was hyphenated Berry-Strawberry. Margarita Anne had the greatest potential of becoming Margarita Anne Berry-Strawberry-Remus.

During the interview both Ed and Margarita Anne were in high spirits. They kept talking and laughing what it would be like to go golfing in Vancouver, the lotus city of Canada. No person on earth, even Ed's mother, could prevent Ed from getting married until a press conference was about to be called to announce their engagement when Ed's hopes of Margarita Anne becoming his bride was dashed.

Word dribbled out that Margarita Anne was married and worked at the Huff Puff and

Associates attorney's office. She was so frustrated as a legal secretary that she would do almost anything in order to go golfing in Vancouver.

Hearing that Ed had failed to have Margarita Anne as a bride his mother anxiously said, "Ed, what sort of a man are you who can easily find houses to sell but can't find a mate? How will you face death when it comes without procreating a son or daughter?"

It's unthinkable that you remain single for the rest of your life so instead of sending money to the TV evangelists let's attend a church service on Sunday and I'll put $100 in the collection basket and our prayers may be answered."

"Good idea, Mom," Ed replied, "I believe if things go a stray an angel will come to show the way."

Ed believed in prayer, saints, miracles, angels and reincarnation but not in hula hoops, ghosts and unidentified flying objects. The following Sunday Ed accompanied his parents to the No Name Universal Church where Reverend Taylor, a bachelor, spent half of his life spreading the message of God's work.

A sign on the front door read:

Pastor: Jim Taylor VNP

The new and improved NO NAME UNIVERSAL CHURCH (Franchise Available - One Week Training Held in Panoka Next Week)

Confessions between 5:00 pm and 6:00 pm each Saturday

Confess 3 sins and the 4th is free

Have your Visa, Master Charge or American Express ready

Every full- moon there's a blockbuster deal. Confess all your sins and you have one-year to pay with no interest charge
All Individual Sins Kept Strictly Confidential
Free stress test upon request
The church bulletin at the time was appropriate because it read: "Don't let worry kill you – let the church help."

As a member of the parish pulled lustily at the bell-rope parishioners from all walks of life entered the church wearing their Sunday best clothing. The women however, including Misty Park, a friend of the Reverend's friend, because of the Sabbath sunshine appeared prettier than on week days.
As one entered the church the ushers asked, "Do you want a smoking or non-smoking pew?"
The Bible used in the church on this occasion was the Dr. Seuss version which professed the creed that there was only one God.

Pastor Taylor's homily that Sunday was going to be about Chasing Rainbows.
The Reverend however, when he entered the pulpit, dressed in his finest vestments, delivered a sermon in ten minutes, half the usual length of his regular sermons.
In a melancholy voice he explained, "Dear parishioners, I regret to inform you that my dog, which is fond of eating paper, ate that portion of my sermon which I was unable to give this morning."

Ed enjoyed the cheerful hymns that were sung by the Gospel Choir and afterward the organ that pealed forth as parishioners filed out where at the front door Ed shook hands with the Revered Taylor and cautiously said, "Pastor, if that dog which you mentioned has pups, I sure would like to get one for my mother."

Minutes later the Reverend introduced Ed to Misty who had a cosmic secret that brought all the promises of the Law of Attraction. Shirley had sparkling eyes, was rather slim and short in stature but gorgeous looking.

After the couple had a chit-chat Misty agreed to be Ed's date at a forthcoming Halloween masked party.

One should know more about the No Name Universal Church in Edmonton. It allows women as ministers and couples getting married can invent their own vows. Parishioners after each service are encouraged to play bingo in the basement as soon as the service is over. The service itself is a gathering, fashion show and a circus all rolled into one. There are four types of church goers and like in most churches' their pecking order can be gleamed from the choice of pews with respect to the distance from the altar. The devout worshippers and those in wheel chairs like to occupy the front seats.

Volunteers are ushers and assist with the offertory, collection and point out where the washrooms are situated. The humble folks come early to ensure themselves a seat in the back rows. Shy, they favor this part of the church as not to be seen yet able to see everybody and everything in front of them. For people who arrive just in time or late, there are rows of empty seats in the middle of the church waiting to be filled and then it's not hard to hear the clickity click clatter of their heels on the tiled floor with children in tow.

Regardless if all the pews are taken or not there are always parishioners who prefer standing in the fringes. They drift

near the entrances and outside within hearing distance
from the strategically located sound speakers. They are
referred to as "Outstanding" members of the church and
compromise the fourth group in the short list. As the
largest group, they consist of many interesting characters.
Among them are the 'Deep Boys'. They come in late
and leave ahead of everyone else. It seems they hardly
have time to hear the entire service but show up just the
same only to fulfill his/her duty. Few venture to kneel
at the pew, bow their heads in silent prayer and depart
quietly. Occasionally one can find their direct opposite.
They are there before the service begins and remain in the
church long after everyone has left. More than not, they
are there for a special reason: to light a candle or Devine
intervention. They like Jack Horner kneel in one corner
and are oblivious the *Bible* being read. Still others in the
fourth group are sweet hearts or looking for a mate. To
them the church is an assembly area to congregate and
date. They opt to stand by the entrances where it is easier
to spot a potential mate or friend as soon as they enter or
leave.

There was a time when rubber shoes, miniskirts, jeans
and sleeveless T shirts with an *Eskimo* or *Oiler* on them
would cause eyebrows, Of late, however new fasion trends
and relaxing of standards has encouraged Pastor Taylor to
preach while members of the church are wearing sandals,
high heel shoes, shorts, blouses with a cleavage showing,
miniskirts, hot pants and T shirts with photos of either the
Eskimos' or *Oilers'*.

Teenagers have greatly been infected by the fashion
revolution. Before advent of the karaoke singing in the
church was the only excuse to sing in public. Everyone now

sings lustily and with spirited gusto. During Christmas and Easter they sing with hands clapping and feet tapping. Trouble is that everyone likes to sing either an octave higher or lower. Thank goodness there is no rapping yet doing the *Lord's Prayer* although there are a drum and a flute to compliment the church organ.

The No Name Universal Church in Edmonton is new in history and home of pigeons and magpies. They nest in the rafters, crevices and nooks above. Their cheerful chirping as they hop and flutter over the chandeliers brighten rather than diminish the solemnity of the service as the birds on occasion drop dung on one's head or shoulder.

When Halloween night arrived Ed and Misty attended a swanky charity masked party at the Petroleum Club. Ed had purchased new costumes for each but on the night of the party Misty claimed she had a terrible headache and said, "Ed, you go to the party alone."
Ed protested vehemently but Misty argued and said she was going to take some aspirin and rest. "There's no need of your good times being spoiled by not going," she said. Ed finally relented, took his costume and went to the party. Misty on the other hand after sleeping soundly for an hour, awakened with out pain and as it was still early decided to go to the party also. In as much as Misty did not know the costume Ed was wearing she thought she would have some fun watching Ed's demeanor and how he acted at a time when Misty wasn't with him.
Misty who never quite got over her childish habit of talking to her self, said, "I best join the party," and thought she spotted Ed cavorting on the dance floor, dancing with every female he could, planting a kiss here and there.

Eventually Misty a seductive babe herself sidled up to Ed and there were more kisses and touches exchanged.

Just before unmasking at midnight Misty slipped away, went to Ed's condo, put her
costume away and got wondering what kind of an explanation Ed would make for his behavior.
Misty was still reading a magazine in the living room when Ed came home and she with perfunctory solitude asked, "What kind of a time did you have, dear?"
"You know, I didn't have a good time because you weren't with me."
"Did you dance much?"
"I never danced even one dance."
"How come?"
"Because when I got to the party I met other real estate salesmen. We went into a den and played poker all evening. But I'll tell you something."

"What?"
"The guy I loaned my costume to sure had a good time."

Realizing that Misty could not be trusted Ed lost interest in her and two days later met Stella who had grown up in the town of Smoky Lake.
There is more to Smoky Lake, an hour drive northeast from Edmonton, than the Government Tree Farm, the Farmer's Senior's Curling Bonspiel and an occasional Tupperware party. There's the Annual October Pumpkin Festival where competitors compete in growing the largest pumpkin in Alberta.
With magnificent weather that day a pumpkin was placed in the back seat of the car and while driving along Highway

28 with Stella by his side headed to the platform where the pumpkins were being weighed.

Stella's pumpkin had potential as a ring of competitors watched her lift the vegetable and it dropped to the ground in full force and split open.

Stella had raised her pumpkin to 150 pounds. Mind you this is not big deal because pumpkins in Nova Scotia had grown to 1000 pounds at the World Pumpkin Weigh-In. Stella's pumpkin was the largest grown by farmers and gardeners in the province of Alberta..

At any rate Stella went to work and scooped the pumpkin remains into a plastic garbage bag for the Pumpkin Weigh-In chairman to weigh.

"Looks like your pumpkin has exploded," the chairman said.

"It may have exploded but it's still a pumpkin. Please weigh it," Stella insisted but the chairman refused and subsequently the Pumpkin-Weigh-In committee agreed with chairman's ruling.

The trip to Smoky Lake did not have a happy ending because on the way back to Edmonton there was a thunder storm ahead of them and a romance did not begin when Stella admitted that her husband practiced polygamy and she was one of his five wives.

During the month of December Ed discovered Norma who prior to Christmas Eve both celebrated the holiday like children listening to the latest Christmas hits on the radio which included: *Grandma Was Run Over by Rudolf the Reindeer, Our Turkey Died of Fright On Christmas Eve* and *Ogopogo Is Pulling Santa's Sleigh This Christmas Eve.*

Ed bought a tree at Zellers and Norma helped him decorate it. Then they as a couple placed their presents at the foot of the tree gift wrapped with multi colored paper and ribbons. On Christmas Eve Ed and Norma attended a midnight service at the No Name Universal Reformed Church and listened to Reverend Taylor tell an ancient story of Emperor Augustus's personal decree on how the world became taxed.

Norma still had not paid her income tax for that year. Feeling alarmed she returned to her boarding house to fill out a Revenue Canada form. Ed didn't see Norma again until the following Easter holidays.

On Boxing Day Ed didn't shop for block buster discount blow-out specials but continued his quest to find a bride believing that he was cursed. Since there weren't many real estate sales made during this period Ed decided to do some skiing in Jasper National Park. In denial Ed learned that it wasn't a curse but a blessing when he met Esther and they became intimately involved with gravity and downhill skiing.

As soon as Ed and Esther put on their skis they headed for the nearest lift.

At the top of the snow-covered mountain the runs were so steep that mountain goats were seen wearing seat belts.

The shorter steep red run was the one which Esther wanted both to take but Ed wasn't a good skier. In the end it was agreed that Ed would take the long easy black run and Esther the short steep red run which had many moguls, and that they would meet at the lodge in one hour.

After one-hour of skiing Ed headed straight for the lodge and waited for Esther at a window seat enjoying a cup of coffee.

As Ed was enjoying his coffee he kept watching the mountain slopes because surely, any moment Esther would join him. But she hadn't until a ski patrol toboggan brought her down and Esther was unconscious.

When an ambulance arrived and took Esther to Emergency at the Jasper Hospital a waiting doctor said, "We'll have to take Esther for an x-ray."

The x-ray showed that Esther had split her head open when blinded by a snow storm her skis caught a snowdrift and she in turn struck a tree. Esther wasn't able to ski for at least another season, if at all.

Ed had a deadline to meet so his romance with Esther discontinued but a new one began with the beautiful nurse that was taking care of her. Her name was Gloria.

Gloria had every shade of blue in her sparkling eyes and a curvaceous body. Before graduating from the University Of Alberta Nursing School she had gone to a finishing one in Basel, Switzerland. In a days time that Ed had known Gloria he was swinging from chandeliers and asked if she wanted to meet his parents in Edmonton. Unknown to Gloria Ed desperately wanted Gloria to be his wife.

Gloria said, 'Why not?" and then asked, "Are your parents rich?"

"They aren't but my uncle Saint Anthony is. His income from stocks and bonds along with his regular and old age pensions is the talk of the town and many widows want to change their name to his."

Neighbors called Anthony 'Saint Anthony' because his name was Anthony and also, perhaps because he had many traits of Anthony of Padua who was canonized in 1232 by Pope Gregory 1X at Spoleto, Italy.

This Anthony like the real saint at one time lived in a cave and swept the nearby Saint Joseph Seminary.

He was, despite his 65 years, a gifted speaker and sympathized with the plight of the Street People, urging them to come before City Council to protest that they were in need of better shelter, food and clothing, so his name "Saint Anthony" had become kind of a proverb.

As soon as Gloria and Ed arrived in Edmonton they entered his parents' home where Ed introduced Gloria to them and then Saint Anthony who took her hand and said, "I'm delighted to meet you."

She acknowledged with "And I'm delighted to meet you too, sir."

Then Saint Anthony said, "I hear that Ed wants to marry you. Is that true?"

Gloria looked at Ed, his parents and then Uncle Saint Anthony.

Second later she said, "Look, this is embarrassing. Please get me out of here."

Ed was stunned, unable to speak as he watched his uncle take Gloria by the arm and walk out the door. A moment later he heard the roar of a Cadillac.

A week later Ed received a telegram from his uncle that read:

"Gloria and I are on a European Honeymoon."

Ed lamented, "The only reason Gloria married you instead of me isn't because she loves you but because she thinks you are rich."

A week later Ed received another telegram. This one signed by Gloria and read:

"Your uncle Anthony died today. Waiting for instructions where to bury him."

Ed notified members of Uncle Anthony's immediate family.

First she was his sidekick and a short time later a possible mate. Josephine was an avid reader and rather vain and a frivolous character.

Josephine was a beautiful Polish foreign contract worker employed by Jimmy the Greek fast food restaurant at West Edmonton Mall. Her contract was about to expire and having read the sport pages a great deal on her day off she said, "Ed, I have been in Canada nearly two years and never been to its national sport, a hockey game. Before I return to Poland, let's take in a game between the Edmonton Oilers and the Calgary Flames."

That's an excellent idea," Ed said and while at Rexall Place the same evening Edmonton fans were cheering from the right and those favoring Calgary from the left. While by sheer accident Josephine and Ed were seated in the middle. Each group came armed with all sorts of noise-making devices that included cowbells, sirens and whistles to cheer their favorite team on to victory often yelling "Go! Go! Go! - One, two, three four, who are we for?"

Josephine and Ed had to twist their heads from one end of the arena to the other following the puck.

Josephine said she was familiar with the names of several National Hockey League stars which included Sydney Crosby, Wayne Gretzky, Mark Messier, Bobby Orr, Maurice Richard, Gordie Howe, Bobby Hull and she even read about Howie Meeker, Don Cherry, Cyclone Taylor, Newsy Lalonde and the Cook and Boucher brothers.

Although Josephine never had attended a hockey game during her entire life she was exited by being able to witness the rivalry between Edmonton and Calgary in the 'Battle' of Alberta.

"Soccer is the favorite sport in Poland," she said

It was near the end of the game at a time the Oilers were hot and the Flames not and while Edmonton was leading 4-3 a sudden fist-fight erupted between two rugged opposing defensemen and seconds later all the players on the ice from each team dropped their gloves including the two goaltenders.

The players were using explicit language while punching, pushing, crashing and wrestling each other. There was hockey gear including helmets and hockey sticks scattered over the ice surface when Josephine disapprovingly said, "Ed, in hockey fighting seems more popular than chasing the puck."

"That's the Canadian way," Ed said and believed fighting was permissible during a NHL game.

Showing displeasure Josephine assertively said, "Fighting? If I want to see fighting I can watch Wrestlemania on TV. The game of hockey is too rough for me, let's get out of here!"

Since Josephine felt fighting should be disallowed and the ruled changed, Ed on the other hand had no appetite to have the rule eliminated and thus their dating discontinued.

Ed had one consolation however; he had won the 50-50 draw.

On their way out of Rexal Place Ed asked Josephine about her broken English.

"For a foreign woman you think English is easy, huh? Read this list I have with me if you still think so, Josephine replied, The list with the same spelling but a different meaning was as follows:

1. The bandage was wound around the wound
2. The farm was used to produce produce

3. The dump was full that it had to re<u>fuse t</u>he re<u>fuse</u>
4. We must po<u>lish t</u>he Po<u>lish f</u>urniture
5. He could le<u>ad if</u> he could get the le<u>ad o</u>ut
6. The soldier decided to de<u>sert the</u> de<u>sert</u>
7. Since there was no time like the pr<u>esent</u>, he thought it was time to <u>present</u> the <u>present</u>
8. A ba<u>ss w</u>as pained on the b<u>ass dr</u>um
9. When shot at, the <u>dove dove</u> into the bushes
10. I did not ob<u>ject to</u> the ob<u>ject</u>
11. The insurance policy was inv<u>alid fo</u>r the inv<u>alid</u>
12. There was a row <u>amo</u>ng the oarsmen about how to row
13. They were too clo<u>se to</u> the door to clo<u>se it</u>
14. The buck doe<u>s fu</u>nny things when the doe<u>s are</u> present
15. A seamstress and a sew<u>er fe</u>ll into the sew<u>er line</u>
16. To help with planting, the farmer thought his <u>sow</u> to <u>sow</u>
17. The win<u>d wa</u>s too strong to win<u>d the</u> sail
18. Upon hearing the tear <u>I </u>shed a tear
19. I had to sub<u>ject the</u> sub<u>ject to</u> series of tests
20. How can I int<u>imate to</u> my most int<u>imate fr</u>iends?

"Indeed the English language can be strange," Ed replied.

"Gung Hat Fat Cho!" (Happy New Year) Ed said as soon he disassociated himself with Josephine and welcomed Sandy who was a dancer he had met before. A large crowd gathered in Edmonton's Chinatown. First a large dragon swayed back and forth along 97th Street, chasing a red rooster. Following the dragon there were people playing drums and gons, and lion dancers with paper lion heads on sticks. As the parade proceeded, store and business owners came outside to give the dancers money. As Ed had already spent most of his while skiing in Jasper he gave Sandy a two-pound roll of baloney instead.

Chinese New Year's Day is celebrated as a family affair, a time for friends, reunion and thanksgiving.

After the parade and fireworks ended Sandy and Ed went to Sandy's home where they sat around a stove, ate a fortune cookie and cracked jokes. In the process Sandy ate the entire baloney roll and soon had a bloated stomach. Not feeling well Sandy then called her mother.

Seeing her daughter's stomach bulging her mother thought Sandy was pregnant and with her hands clenched into fists indignantly screamed, "God have mercy daughter, look the shape you are in! How could you be so blind and disgrace our family?"

Sandy was taken by the arm and sent to her bedroom.

Ed thought he had learned a lesson: If one is full of baloney he/she should keep their mouth shut.

Since Ed still had not found a suitable mate this concerned his parents, especially his mother who suggested that Ed go to the Bissell Food Bank on 96th Street and there would be lineup of poor and destitute men and women seeking food hampers and clothes to wear.

"Surely in the line-up you'll notice a mate potential," his mother said.

Ed never experienced hunger or pain and did as told. He had not known anyone in the 2-block long lineup and was lucky when on a harsh cold winter day when it began getting dark at 4:00 p.m. caught the attention of a stunningly beautiful Anita.

Anita wore a wrinkled blue dress under a red parka and looked graceful and innocent, not at all like some of the other girls who worked the nearby streets and intersections.

It was Ed's destiny to have dinner with Anita the following day at a nearby Vietnamese e restaurant. Anita wore the same wrinkled dress when they met a day before. Up close she was even more captivating than when he saw her earlier. Anita had the most beautiful eyes he had ever seen. Her cascading black hair flowed onto her shoulders.

She wore no makeup, was shy, pensive and reserved and barely said a word all that night but seemed to know that she was a special person on a special occasion and possibly Ed's bride. Anita did not eat much however, and that night asked for her food to be bagged to go so that she could share it with her mother.

Over the next several evenings Anita and Ed met again and on one occasion Anita was full of surprises and asked for Ed's picture.

"Sorry but I didn't bring any," Ed said but if you wish we'll go shopping tomorrow afternoon and I'll have one taken."

"That would be kind of you."

When Ed and Anita went shopping Anita took him to Goodwill, Salvation Army Thrift Store and Value Village to purchase subsidized clothing. They were stores favored by the poor and homeless.

Ed gave Anita his photograph and wanted to buy her something more uplifting. At Holt Renfrew he purchased a designer dress whose price was $135.

When they left HR Anita was all smiles, overjoyed with the fancy shopping bag in her hand.

In parting Anita said, "Thank you for your picture and a wonderful present. I'll be wearing it tomorrow night when we meet again."

But the following night Anita stood Ed up and when they met the following night he asked the reason.

Anita replied, "Because yesterday my mother took the dress back to Holt Renfrew to get the money instead."

A tear ran down Anita's cheek. She paused silently for several seconds and then said. "My mother said I could not have the dress because we didn't have enough food to eat."

Ed said that the dress was no big deal and Anita had no reason to be upset.

"I'll buy you another dress."

As Ed was about the sweep Anita off her feet she held back and after pensive pause while wiping her tears replied, "Thanks a lot. I can't live with that but I shall never forget your offer. I first must work myself through the endurable poverty my mother and I are in, and then we can meet again."

Ed was bewildered. As it turned out Ed and Anita did not meet again but during a still colder evening Ed believed Reverend Taylor could spiritually support him in reaching his dream to find a life-long loving mate.

CHAPTER 5

Pastor Taylor and Ed met in Ed's condo Saturday evening and after discussing Ed's search, which was floundering, they played cards, mostly cribbage, and enjoyed several bottles of beer. During the conversation Taylor said he was nervous about a homily he was preparing for Sunday's service.

"Relax," Ed said, "It may help if you take some beer home with you. After a bottle or two everything should go smoothly. Here take a dozen home with you."

On Sunday morning Ed went to church and Reverend Taylor felt great. He was able to talk up a storm using Ed's suggestion. However, upon completion of the service and returning to the rectory Reverend Taylor found this note from Ed:

Dear Reverend Taylor, my friend,
Even clergy can have off days.
I said a bottle or two of beer not a dozen.
There are Ten Commandments not twelve.
There are twelve disciples, not ten.
We do not refer to the cross as, "The Big T."
The recommended grace before a meal is not necessarily, "Rub-a-dub-dub, thanks for the grub. Just say, "Pa, ta."

We do not refer to our savior Jesus Christ to as, "J. C. and the boys."

When David slew Goliath, he did not use a machine gun, it was a slingshot."

The Father, the Son and the Holy Spirit are not referred to as "Big Daddy, Junior and Spook."

It's always the Virgin Mary, never Mary with a cherry

Next Wednesday there will be taffy pulling contest at the No Name Universal Reformed Church and not a Peter-pulling contest at Saint Taffy's.

Last but not least, the title of the Book is The Holy Bible and not, "Our Sexy Savior's Saucy Story."

The following day during Ed's busy life he received a seductive phone call from Pearl to list her bungalow for sale. Ed initially thought Pearl could be a candidate to be a mate but then when they met discovered she had died earlier and reincarnated as a paranormal striking ghost, he changed his mind. Pearl was large in stature, a pale quiet woman with heavy eyelids over weak eyes. Her hair turned red or blond as candle lights fell on it. She wore black clothes, was pigeon toed and had a long nose.

The five room dingy home was old and in need to have repair. The floor was filthy, the windows were black with grime and the bathroom toilet was overflowing.

When Ed arrived the weather forecasters were wrong. Instead of sunshine there was a snow storm outside and with a restless wind, every gust made noise beyond telling. The snow and wind splashed and gurgled as the poplar trees nearby swayed back and forth rattling and roaring. After measuring each room Pearl walked through a wall while walking from the kitchen to the living room. Ed did not believe in ghosts until while following Pearl;

struck the same wall but didn't get through like Pearl did, injuring his nose.

Pearl then was the talk of the town not that she had her house for sale but because of her lobbying the Alberta legislature to commemorate the historical ghost towns in Alberta including Little Chicago, Alberta where she was born.

Ed also dealt with who he thought was a tramp. This occurred on Jasper Avenue in front of Ed's condo where a female identified herself as Natasha who said she was blind and asked, "Any beer, wine or pop bottles or cans, sir?"

"Do I look like some one who drinks liquor so early in the morning?" Ed replied.

"I also collect vinegar bottles but perhaps you could spare some change for a cup of coffee?"

Ed handed Natasha a $1:00 coin and in the process it fell to the ground. Natasha picked it up which prompted Ed to say. "My dear lady, but you aren't blind."

"I know sir," Natasha replied, "I'm working for my brother who is and enjoying his holidays in Hawaii"

After a short flirtation conversation Ed felt that he and Natasha had little in common therefore it would be a pointless exercise to date her. The lady however, did have some advice for Ed when she said, "Mr. Remus, I have a retirement plan."

"Oh ya, tell me more."

"Well, Mr. Remus, if one had purchased $1000 of Nortel stock one year ago, it would now be worth $49.00.

With Evron you would have had $16.50 left of the original $1000.

With WorldCom, you would have had less than $5.00 left.

If you purchased $1000.00 of Delta Airlines stock you would have had $49.00 left.

But if you had purchased $1000 of wine one year ago, drank all the wine, then turned in the bottles for a recycling REFUND you would d have had $214.00.

Based on this knowledge, the best current advice is to drink heavily and recycle."

Next Ed dated Vicky and as the dating process proceeded everything was fine until Ed discovered Vicky was a victim of Winter Blues whose symptoms included daytime drowsiness, night time fatigue, diminished concentration, feeling of misery, guilt, a sudden loss of esteem and a tendency to avoid social contact. It would have been romantic if Vicky and Ed looked at the stars. But stars are rarely seen in Edmonton during a snow storm and the temperature reaches -30C degrees.

Ed however, was willing to continue dating Vicky but then he discovered that the Winter Blues disorder is related to the secretion of the hormone melatonin, a sleep related secretion by the pineal gland of the brain. This hormone is believed to cause symptoms and is produced at increased levels in the dark. As the summer months in Edmonton are short and winter months long Ed did not give in to winter bla's. He could not see himself married to one whose mood cycles varied during each month so he discontinued seeing Vicky.

On Valentine's Day Ed was invited to an office party where he met Blossom, a possible mate candidate, and gave her a heart-shaped box of chocolates. The following day Ed offered to take Blossom to go shopping at the Bay but she preferred Independent Jewelers. When Ed

offered to take her to see the movie *Fiddler on the Roof*
she wanted to see *The Sound of Music.*

The bottom line was that Ed found Blossom kind of picky
and he didn't have a clue how to begin a romance with this
pretty woman.

"Blossom is like a weather forecaster," Ed said. "One
day there is sunshine, next a thunder storm and then a
tornado. Her moods are like climate changes and more
complex than *Pokemon* and more of them than *Beanie
Babies.* Its something I can't contend with in my real
estate profession."

After Ed said, 'Good-bye' to Blossom it was, 'Move over
Diane', who was beautiful but haughty, conceited and
had a fiery temper. After dating Diane for a week Ed
discovered she was a long time member of the Scientology
faith established in 1950 by science fiction writer L. Ron
Hubbard. Scientology opposes medical exams for new
born and according to the tenants of faith known as
Dianetics, words, even loving ones, spoken during the
birth and other painful times are recorded by the 'reactive
mind' are subconscious. Those memories, adherents feel,
can eventually trigger problems for mother and child.

Ed, a real estate conversationist, couldn't make such a
promise and suggested to Diane:

"Promise me that the next time you and I discuss
Scientology and you get angry I suggest you will take a
deep breath and count to 100 before you speak."

Diane slugged Ed over the head with a Ouija board. By
the time she counted to 75 Ed had the happiness of seeing
Diane jump into a waiting taxi and drive out of sight.

Ed had planted a rose earlier and watered it faithfully. Before it blossomed he carefully examined it and saw the bud that would soon bloom.

Noticing thorns upon the stem Ed thought, "How can a beautiful flower come from a plant burdened with so many sharp thorns?"

Because of his busy schedule in dealing with real estate matters and searching for a mate at the same time Ed neglected to water the rose, and just before it was ready to bloom, it died.

The following day Ed phoned Stan Thompson a local gardening and plant expert wondering why the plant had died.

Thompson replied, "Look Ed, it's the same with people. Within every soul there's a rose.

The God-like qualities planted in us at birth, grow amid the thorns of our faults. Many look at ourselves and see only the thorns, the defects. We despair, thinking that nothing good can come from us.

We neglect to water the good within us, and eventually it dies.

We never realize our potential. Some people do not see the rose within themselves; someone else must show it to them.

One of the greatest gifts a person can possess is to be able to reach past the thorns of another, and find the rose within them. Why don't you ask Reverend Taylor and see in which direction your career is heading?"

The following Sunday Ed and Pastor Taylor, an expert in many theological subjects, sat at a table in his rectory and Ed asked the question: "Reverend Taylor, my real estate career is okay but my search for a mate isn't. In your candid opinion despite my success and failure, can you tell me where in my life am I heading?"

Clergyman Taylor as Ed's spiritual counselor felt he couldn't help and suggested that as an oncoming realtor he should contact Saint Rose in Heaven who while living on Planet Earth lived a life of austerity and had already performed major miracles in favor of Canada. The saint had already performed two miracles in Canada by preventing the province of Quebec from separating from rest of Canada and Canada not becoming the 51st state of United States.

Appearing on Ed's computer screen Saint Rose began by saying, "Ed, I have been watching you down below and it has come to my attention that you now sell taller buildings and have a shorter temper, travel on wide freeways, but have a narrower viewpoint; you spend more, but have less, you buy more but what you buy enjoy less.

You sell bigger houses with smaller families; more conveniences but less time. You have more 'Best Seller' awards but less sense; more knowledge, but less judgment. Best Sellers Realty employs more salesmen but it has more problems.

I notice too that you haven't learned how to swim yet and drink too much, spend too recklessly, laugh too little, drive too fast, get angry too quickly, stay up too late, get up too tired, read too little, watch TV too much and pray too seldom.

It appears to me that you talk too much, love too seldom, and hate too often. You've learned how to make a comfortable living, but not a comfortable life. You have added years to life, not life to years.

"Ed, from now on you'll have to change your ways.
Those on Planet Earth have been all the way to the moon and back but you seem to have trouble crossing the hallway to meet your new condo neighbors. Outer space has been conquered but you haven't conquered your inner space. You've done large things but you haven't done better things and still can't swim.

At the suggestion of Sarah you've cleaned up the kitchen in your condominium but polluted your soul. By being naught with several of your potential mates. Scientists have split the atom but you haven't your prejudice. You write more deals but earn less. And you plan more but accomplish less. How come?

Ed, I realize you are looking for an everlasting mate and learned to rush but not to wait. You have a higher income but lower morals.
These are the days of two incomes and more SUV's but more divorces; of fancier houses but broken homes. Especially in Edmonton there are a lot of stabbings and gun-related gangs.
These are the days of quick trips, disposable diapers, throw away morality, one night stands, overweight bodies and pills that do everything from cure, to quiet and to kill. And Ed, you are asking where are you heading?
Well, let me tell you. If your mother dies before you find a wife she can not be replaced and you will feel the loss for the rest of your life."
After a short pause Saint Rose continued, "You were not made to last for ever, and God wants you to be in Heaven with Him. This is your dress rehearsal. God wants you to practice on earth what you will do forever in eternity. Life is a series of problems as you are in one now. You

are reasonably happy on earth, but that should not be your
goal in life. Your goal should be to grow in character, in
Christ likeness.

With that premise in mind Ed hooked up with Norma
the second time and as Easter approached he and Norma
celebrated the holiday as if it was Christmas holiday time.
Ed had a lot of unpacking to do, unpack the Christmas
tree and decorate it with Easter lights which were multi
colored and shaped like Easter eggs.
Pussy willows and oh-so-adorable bunnies were used to
decorate the tree. Mind you many of the bunnies were
made of plastic imported from China where labor making
such things was cheep, much cheaper than in Canada or
America.
While decorating the tree Ed and Monica sat by candlelight
and listened to the radio and the latest releases a disc
jockey on Rock 97 FM hadn't played before including:
Rapping n *Rolling' with a Bunny, Mummy Forgot to Put
Yeast in the Hot Cross Buns and The Vegreville Easter
Egg is Big but not Bigger than Biggar, Saskatchewan.*

When Easter Day arrived the first thing Ed and Norma
did was to attend a Sunrise Church service and listen to
Reverend Taylor tell an ancient story about a Superior who
died on a cross for those living on Planet Earth.

Although one could not see the sun rising in the horizon
because of fog it was a celebration of a feast of child born
on Christmas day who grew into adulthood and died on a
Friday and rose from the dead on a Sunday.
Then Ed and Norma exchanged Easter presents. Norma
received sweater with a bouquet of red tulips and a card
that read: "Norma you can be my mate frisky as a filly."

Ed did not receive a gift or flowers as Norma turned in her friendship ring and left a card which read: "Ed, you have been naughty since I began dating you and here's the scoop. All you get for Easter this year is my farewell and the Snowman's poop."

CHAPTER 6

Ed was about to give up hope in his search for a mate until he met Rachael at the Kingsway Garden Mall. Rachael was the daughter of a Revenue Canada tax collector who had been dead several years and the mother hoped to find a husband for her daughter. They had moderate means and were an honorable, gentle, quiet couple.

Rachael was weighted with diamonds and Ed believed she was a perfect type of the virtuous women who men dream of one day intrusting their happiness.

Her simple beauty had the modesty, charm and an imperceptible smile which constantly hovered reflection of a pure, honest and lovely soul. Ed thought he could not find a better wife.

Ed was unspeakably happy dating Rachael but then in the second week she stole his heart and credit card when she charged up all sorts of jewelry and gems, and while smilingly one day said, "Look Ed, are they not lovely?"

On receiving a bill with 18% interest to pay, Ed was beside himself. He was astonished and now in considerable debt, wished time for reflection.

The theft caused Ed much sorrow. He thought once, twice and even thrice while overcome with fatigue. Ed then called police and Rachael was charged with theft of over $10,000.

After Ed paid his account he received a bill for his unused
credit card stating that he still owed $0.00. He ignored
it and threw the notice away. A month later Ed received
another bill and threw that one away too. The following
month the credit card company sent him a nasty note
stating they were going to cancel his credit card if he
didn't send $0.00 by return mail. Ed called the credit
card company and talked with an officer who said it was
a computer problem and he would take care of it.

The following month Ed decided it was about time he
tried out the troublesome credit card figuring that if there
were purchases on his account it would put an end to the
ridiculous predicament. However, in the first store that he
produced his credit card in payment for his purchases he
found that the credit car had been cancelled. He called
the credit card company who apologized for the computer
error once again and an officer said he would take care of
it but the following day he got a bill for $0.00 stating that
the payment was now due.

Assuming that having spoken to the credit card company
only the previous day the latest bill was another mistake
so he ignored it, trusting the company would be as good
as their word and sort the problem out. The following day
however, he got a bill for $0.00 stating that he had ten
days to pay his account or the company would have to
take steps to recover his debt.

Finally Ed gave in and thought he would play the company
at its own game and mailed it a cheque for $0.00. The
computer duly processed the account and returned a
statement to Ed that he now owed the credit card company
nothing. A week later Ed's bank called him asking what

he was doing writing a cheque for $0.00? After a lengthy explanation the bank replied that the $0.00 cheque had caused their processing software to fail. The bank now could not process ANY cheque from ANY of its customers that day because the cheque for $0.00 was causing the computer to crash.

The following month Ed received a letter from the credit card company claiming that his cheque had bounced and that he now owned it $0.00 and unless he sent a cheque by return mail it would take steps to recover the debt.
As far as Ed knows the credit company is still trying.

It was while Ed was in his office that he received a phone call from Jimmy Cane living on a farm near Saint Albert who said, "Ed, will you please come and appraise our farm. I shall be delighted if you will."
Ed accepted the invitation with a promise that the Cane daughter, Charity, would hold the measuring tape for him.
An hour later Ed set off in his car to the backwoods where the farm was situated.
On his way to evaluate the farm Ed found a bridge over a stream washed away due to a torrential rain storm in the area.
Ed noticed a farmer nearby watching ducks swimming back and forth so he asked the farmer, "How deep is the stream? Do you think I can drive through with my car?"
"I believe you can," the farmer replied and Ed began driving through it, however, the car sank in the middle and he barely escaped with his life.
"What do you mean telling me I could cross the stream? The stream is at least six feet deep," Ed said.
The farmer scratched his head. "Funny," he said. "It only reaches to the middle of the ducks."

The farmer eventually got his tractor and pulled Ed's car out of the stream. Ed listed the Cane farm for sale and left Charity a calling card with his photo on it at the same time. Unfortunately Ed did not meet Charity that day because the car was stalled due to the sparkplugs being wet.

He did not meet Charity the next day either nor the day after that, as during that time she had gone to the Olds Agricultural College in southern Alberta to take a crash course in husbandry.

"Ah shucks. I'm disappointed. I wonder who is kissing her now," Ed said and following day hooked up with Marie and after his work day was done helped her filling out coupons found in shopping malls, newspapers and magazine and those conducted on the radio and television.

In a short while Marie had over 10,000 entries for various contests and although she had sore lips from licking envelopes, she won hundreds of cans of veggies, pasta, cheese and dried fruit which began to pile up in her apartment on 124th Street.

"What am I going to do what all that food? I have no room to breathe. It's a shame to have all this food to go to waste," Marie said anxiously.

"Why don't you compact them into pill form and then you'll have all the space you need," Ed suggested.

"An excellent idea," Marie said and with Ed's help took the cans and packages into the kitchen where Marie ran the contents trough a meat grinder and then a food processor.

Next Marie laid out the concoction on a table and with a rolling pin, rolled out the ingredients thin. A cookie cutter was used to have the concentrated food made into pill into form. This done, the pills were put into the stove oven to dehydrate.

Once out of the oven, each pill, the size of a Canadian dollar coin, and containing nourishment for an entire day, was placed into a refrigerator where Marie said, "There, no more food that will be wasted. It's in pill form now and all that is needed is a bit of water to sustain life."
Marie even looked forward to market the pill as a new concept in the fast food industry but it had its drawbacks compared to a pizza or even the Big Mac.

The following morning, while alone and enjoying the new discovery for breakfast, Marie was impressed with the pill's small size, containing a pound of concentrated nourishment but the pill she was enjoying soon got lodged in her throat causing Marie to cough and choke.
Marie slapped herself across her back but it had little effect. Seeing a glass of water beside her Marie swallowed a mouthful but this was fatal. The water caused the pill to expand in her stomach and minutes later there was a huge explosion.
You may have heard of the Halifax explosion in 1917. Well, this explosion was just as huge and fragments of Marie's body were found on a farm in the outskirts of Edmonton and the land where the fragments landed turned a luscious green in color.

It is sad to think that Marie, this pretty, vivacious, young woman who would possibly become Ed's bride instead became a piece of fertilizer.

Men are supposed to be hunters, the aggressors of the dating world so during the month of May Ed returned to the Riverside Health Centre where he met Trisha who wasn't divorced, overweight or exposed her cleavage.

Her hair was blond, eyes pale green and skin lily white so pried as she walked about the resort and the nearby North Saskatchewan River.

Trisha appeared self-confident but Ed wasn't certain this charming, foot loose and heart free, young lady from Toronto was a 'good for now' of a woman with wife potential.

To find out Ed invited Trisha for a moonlight walk along the river at a time when crickets and frogs serenaded them and there was a breeze that had a lesson to teach, the waves a story to tell and the moon and stars sing a song of glory that Ed couldn't put into words.

Every woman wants to look alluring. In beauty, as in everything else, there is no level playing field but Trisha had God-given good looks that deserved Ed's attention as she maximized her natural assets.

Ed enjoyed Trisha's company immensely but his father didn't and said, "Love has a tendency for one to be blind. With Trisha you have stumbled on someone who I believe is clear off the radar screen. You would be better off to show Trisha a copy of *Cosmos* where the sun doesn't shine."

Even though Ed did not have his father's consent before he would propose marriage or even buy matching face towels and tooth brushes there were areas of exchange much deeper than a casual conversation about Ed's income. At this point Trisha appeared confused and finally said, "Ed, before we talk about caterers and flower arrangements let's wait a bit longer."

"How long?"

"At least another year."

Ed wasn't prepared to wait that long and sadly replied, "It's now or never. I can't wait that long. One year from now will be too late."

The conversation then took on a new twist when Ed asked, "Why so long?"

"Because I don't know your flaws and you don't know mine. One never knows when a prince may turn into a toad and vice versa."

Gone was a romance that was divine when Ed threw up his hands and groaned; "Ugh, very well. One can lead a horse to water but one can not make it to drink. I'll continue my search and eventually will find another."

Recovering from a broken heart Ed resigned himself that a marriage with Trisha wasn't forthcoming so the search for a bride continued. Ed wanted to get married but at the same time would settle for nothing less than perfection.

Whatever the circumstances, the end of a love affair can be painful so at the suggestion of a former classmate, Louis, Ed went to the Odeon Theatre to relieve his agony and take in movie *Of Men and Mice*. Ed sat in an empty seat next to Eugenia, a Marilyn Monroe-like beauty with caressing blue eyes.

Several days in succession Ed and Eugenia lunched at Eugenia parents' home and while playing cards and drinking tea talked for hours where at one point their conversation dealt with family life and love and she said with a grave face, "Ed, now you know my attitude towards family life and my view as to the sanctity of marriage. I love you but as an unmarried woman I won't live with you. Let's just be friends."

Ed cleared his throat and heaved a sigh. For several seconds there was silence which was broken when Ed said," Just friends, why?"

Eugenia was devout and religious and her conviction would not allow her to, "Live in sin."

Despite making no end of promises Ed did not know what to think or theory to adopt so he softly drawled, "Very well. That's how the cookie crumbles."

To this day it's a mystery why Eugenia did not want to live with this handsome, intelligent real estate salesman at a time when it was a common practice that when marriage was forsaken many couples lived common-law.

And it's still a mystery that ranks at par with the disappearance in America of Teamster Union boss Jimmy Hoffa, what happened to Ed's next date, Salome. Salome was a beautiful young Philippine lady Ed had met at a Visayas basement party in Edmonton.

You may not believe and think it's one's imagination, but Salome originally came from the province of Mindanao where *aswang* are the most feared supernatural creatures on the 7001 islands. Te exact number depends if there is a high tide or not.

They can enter the body of a person and through this person they inflict harm on those they dislike. Ed had no idea why anyone would dislike the petit Salome when upon short notice she returned to the island to be at her parent's 50th wedding anniversary.

Most common aswang are the female variety that appear as an ugly old woman with long, unkempt hair, blood-shot eyes, long finger nails, and a long thread-like black tongue.

But the most striking trait of this creature is her ability as a self-segmenter, is to discard her lower body from the shoulders down, from hips down and also down from her knees. She has holes in her armpits which contain oil.

This gives her power of flight. Seldom does she ride on a broomstick or a carpet. Being of enormous power, an aswang can transform herself into any shape, even inanimate objects. She preys on children, pregnant women and ill people. Once she has overpowered a victim, she takes a bundle of sticks, talahib grass, and rice or banana stalks, and transforms these into a replica of her victim. This replica is sent home while she takes the real person back with her. Upon reaching her home, the replica becomes sick and dies. The victim is then eaten. She is particularly fond of the liver. So Ed was on the run to find another one. Not an aswang but a mate and sought advice from *Dear Abby* who ran a syndicated column in the *Journal*.

It is said that her column is read by more people than any other newspaper column world wide As Ms Abby seemed to know everything about mating Ed gave his best shot and wrote:

Dear Abby,
My mother is suspicious why I can't find a life-time partner is because I'm running around with too many women of questionable character. For instance last night she asked if it was Betty, a mail sorter at the post office, Shirley the cashier at the Sobey's Store or Carol, a server at the Weston Hotel. What should I do?

Abby answered:
Dear Ed,

Cheer up. You may not be fooling around with the women you mentioned but you certainly gave your mother three good reasons to keep an eye on you.

Why don't you consult with a matchmaker? Happy hunting.

Abby,

Since Ed had a frustrating time finding a mate he took Abby's advice and made arrangements to meet a traditional matchmaker whose profession was making a comeback.

The following evening Ed met the elderly, garrulous, toothless widow Ziva Hanna who wasn't pretty, short in stature with wrinkles on her cheeks roughened by hardship which she endured during her life. To avoid the danger of high blood pressure Mrs. Hanna sprinkled flax on her cereal and lived in a small meager two-bedroom white house.

The brown metal roof was rusty, the brick chimney tumbling down, the wooden stairs at the front door all rotting away and over grown with grass. It was the most God-forsaken looking house found on 97th Street. Children playing nearby called the place, "The Old Lady's Freak House."

Mrs. Hanna was happy living in the house and wouldn't live anywhere else and as far as

Ed was concerned a consultation didn't cost a penny.

Supporting herself on crutches Mrs. Hanna at four score and three however, was a wise woman who understood courtship rituals and when she was active in matchmaking interviewed more than 300 singles about dating choices. One may truly say Ziva Hanna in her hey-day was the Edmonton anthropologist of dating.

Mrs. Hanna helped Ed overcome his initial nervousness by handing him a cup of herbal tea, and he to her, his resume, After going over the resume Mrs. Hanna in a hoarse voice said, "Ed, you appear to be an intelligent young man which gals should go for but first let me evaluate several and I will call you."

Since all is not gold that glitters, and beauty is but skin deep," Ed said, "Let's try."

That evening Ed went to his condo and waited for a phone call, which did come as he was having a shower.

He picked up the receiver after the sixth ring and on the other end Hanna said, "Ed, I have found your first date that is willing to meet with you. Vivian is a high profile lady your age, an intelligent doll who reads books, has no life trauma or emotional roller coasting. Can I give Vivian your phone number?"

"Please do."

Within an hour the phone rang again. It was Vivian, the high-profile cupid Mrs. Hanna talked about. Following a brief conversation Ed and Vivian agreed to meet in the lobby of the Westin Hotel where following an exchange of pleasant greetings the couple entered the bar, sat at a table where Ed asked, "Vivian, what would you like to drink?"

"Gin and tonic, please."

When the cocktails arrived Vivian accidentally spilled hers and apologized.

"That's all right. No problem. I'll order another, Hey waiter!" Ed hollered.

After the initial nervousness subsided a three-piece combo began playing and up-tempo tune. Ed and Vivian took to the dance floor and like ballroom dancers their footwork went forward and back, back and forward, dipping and flowing.

Following several more rounds of cocktails and dances Vivian began thrashing her previous dates, made self-deprecating comments about her waistline that made Ed embarrassed.

Following still more exploratory conversation Vivian beamed with delight and came right out and said, "I have already applied for maternity leave. Ed, are you ready?"

"To leave? Any time."

"Not to leave home."

"Then what?"

"To get married."

Ed wasn't prepared for an instant marriage or to march up an aisle without his parents present. Mrs. Hanna's first prospect turned out to be a major disappointment.

The following evening Ed's date didn't turn out much better when Kay, a substitute librarian that was an intellectual without intellect, met Ed in the City of Edmonton Public Stanley Milner Library to read about the state of the real estate market in Canada.

Both were the same age but Ed soon found out that Kay spent nights sleeping in a nearby basement because she couldn't afford public housing.

Kay wasn't scavenging dumpsters or buying her clothing from the Goodwill Thrift Store, but then when she said she was a widow, Ed wasn't interested.

"But only recently as my husband died in a fatal car accident on theWhitemud Freeway," Kay said.

"Marrying a widow hasn't entered my mind," Ed replied.

"That's because you have no experience living with one. A widow, especially if she is young and healthy as I am, can make a lovely bride."

Ed felt there was a stigma attached when a young man marries a widow, especially if one was already five months pregnant, as Kay was.

In the second round Hanna gave Ed the names of three other women: Love, Patience and Prudence. With names like that Ed thought one of them had a strong possibility of becoming a permanent mate and again it did not happen.

First he dated Love but they wouldn't be compatible as a married couple because Love snored when asleep and when awake there was hostility and dislike for each other. After one week Love and Ed agreed not to see each other.

Then Ed dated Patience. Ed as a real estate salesmen had the capacity for waiting. He had the ability to enhance waiting or delay without becoming annoyed or upset or to persevere calmly when faced with difficulty.
Patience however, was totally opposite to Ed's demeanor. When Ed took her to see a movie or when she went to the bank Patience was impatient waiting in a long lineup.
Often she would go to sales in department stores and buy things because of the discount price even though she did not need the article. In searching for a mate one thing on Ed's agenda list was not to get involved with shopaholic and an impatient woman.

Finally upon Mrs. Hanna's recommendation Ed dated Prudence who was flirty, always chewed gum and thought she knew everything. Prudence appeared to have a good sense in managing practical matters but since she was a weather forecaster for a local television station her forecasts were always topsy-turvy. Since Canada had Kim Campbell as the first woman prime minister the weather forecasts changed more often than Ed's mother changed her living room furniture. Ed was against women becoming weather forecasters and also a head of a country. He often said, "Take Maier in Israel. Bhutto in Pakistan, Thatcher in Britain and Arroyo in the Philippines, as soon as they gained power there was always turbulence in the weather and the global warming increased. And now with Germany having Merkel as leader the climate changes are more frequent than Elizabeth Taylor changed husbands.

And wait, should Segolene Royal ever becomes president of France and Hillary Clinton of United States; just think of the frequent turbulent storms, tornadoes and hurricanes the world will experience and take a look at the Philippines these days, where Arroyo is in charge, all one hears is about monsoons, one week, mudslides the second, volcanoes, the third, earthquakes the fourth and shipwrecks the next."

With such unpredictable global weather forecasts and Prudence by his side, Ed felt he could not increase his sales.

It was the following evening at a time Ed was enjoying a beer that he felt embarrassed when during darkness an intruder with wings unexpectedly entered his condominium. Puzzled by the home invasion Ed asked the stranger, "And who might you be?" and was told, "I'm your angel Saint Michael."

Skeptical Ed said, "And how did you get here and what is it you want from me, all I have in the fridge is beer to drink."

"I'm doing a Heavenly analysis of your searches for an everlasting mate and determine if you still have to do more suffering before you find your true love. At any rate while I think of it, in Heaven there is no beer so I'll accept your offer to quench my thirst while I'm here."

Handing a bottle with a label marked *Molson's Canadian* Ed continued, "And once you are finished drinking it I'll call police that you leave."

"I wouldn't do that if you want me to help you find an ever lasting loving wife," the angel imperturbably replied at the same time touching Ed on the forehead with his wing. The angel then took a break and replenished his thirst by consuming a second bottle.

Thinking that the angel was a combative alcoholic Ed could not endure the intrusion, even from an angel, became angry, picked up an empty bottle which lay with in his reach and threw it at the angel but the angel dodged or else Ed's aim was inaccurate, breaking the glass of a cuckoo clock hanging on the wall that faced him.

A friendly conversation followed and with considerate kindness of the angel Ed was mollified which led him to ask, "How did you find Edmonton? Las Vegas with its bright lights maybe but Edmonton is the size of a pinhead on the Planet Earth map?"

"Good question. To show the way I followed a star like the one that led the wise men bringing gold, incense and myrrh to baby Jesus in Bethlehem."

Ed was dismayed and about to ask another question, "And..."

"And with the help of the full moon and a back wind I flapped my wings and in no time I was above the clouds and a short later I reached your condominium. Mind you initially it was a bit difficult to find because I'm allergic to chemicals which are harming the environment just north of Edmonton. "

Following more chit-chat the angel apologized and said, "Ed, my time with you is limited as the Angel Department in Heaven is extremely busy and I have other calls to make."

The angel bowed his head, flapped his wings and after shaking hands with Ed on departure, like the time General Douglas MacArthur when Japan occupied the Philippines during World War11, in a gentle and soft voice said, "May God bless you. I shall return."

Since Ed was pacified, he closed the door by which the angel entered, drew the blinds in the bedroom and then said to himself, "Please God help him," and went to sleep.

A day passed and then another and still another and the process of finding a suitable mate remained at a slow pace but Ed wasn't a quitter and stopped at the Greenwood Book Store on 82nd Avenue where book shelves were filled about astrology, numerology. unidentified flying objects and Hollywood celebrities who were undergoing rehabilitation treatment. Ed usually didn't get too excited reading books until he purchased Dr. Phil's *Strategy* which said pets make good companions and walking a dog could stave off depression.

As soon as Ed finished reading the book he got excited and rushed to the SPCA bringing home a German shepherd dog named Windy whose coat suggested fleas and squalor.

Windy put his tail between his legs and howled all night and during the day ran around sniffing and licking all kinds of stuff on the ground.

Windy was a hard working dog however, and the article also said that if trained a dog could sniff out marijuana, cancerous tumors and possibly a mate.

In hopes of finding out Ed took Windy for a walk in Hawerluk Park and struck up smiles and conversations with other pet owners but still failed to find a partner because Windy began eating his own feces thus frightening females away. Aside from being a hard working dog Windy was also clever and used Ed to meet other female dogs.

Although Ed was disappointed he rewarded the dog for his effort with a bone which the pooch chewed voraciously and then disappeared.

Then an idea came to Ed and he rescued a stray cat in the back ally who became his favorite playmate but Kitty needed a bath. Ed thoroughly cleaned the toiled bowl in the bathroom added some soap and put the cat inside, closed the lid and flushed three times. This provided a "power wash and a rinse" which Ed found quite effective. When he lifted the lid the cat jumped out and Ed dried her with a towel.

Following her bath Kitty did not barf hairballs but after several days became a pee stain carpet decorator. Kitty liked to sit on Ed's lap and jump onto his bed and lay at his feet. For his part Ed showed her where she could catch mice.

One day Kitty got into heat and kept making weird 'Meow. Meow' sounds which neighbors found annoying.

The feline had never been fixed and one night Ed opened the door and found a pack of dogs chasing her. That night Kitty died in her sleep an unnatural death.

The following night Ed discovered that he had cockroaches in his condo and that a cockroach is one of the most common creatures capable of inspiring fear instead of love. He was horrified when he saw a dozen roaches which suddenly grew two inches long, slinking across the kitchen floor and the males began to fly at night. They could also swim. When several; climbed up his leg, that is when Ed called Capital City Exterminators for help.

Not many women become pest exterminators but one that did, her name was Rusty.

Rusty wore heavy clothing, wrap-around glasses, a safety orange vest and a respirator. Using a small hand-pumped can she strutted from room to room, corner to corner, and sprayed with a product that sounded like another Schwarzenegger movie, *Killmaster 11*.

Then after Rusty had sprayed the baseboards, cupboards and under the kitchen sink she marked areas where the cockroaches were likely to pass with a poisonous putty-like substance painted green.

As Rusty was cockroach hunting more ran out of the kitchen sink but Rusty gave them a spray and instantly they were dead.

"I was told that pet cockroaches, especially the albino ones, should be treated with respect and a little compassion," Ed said.

"Could be, but on the other hand, cockroaches are notorious harbingers of filth and disease. They leave droppings on their ways that resemble fragments of pencil lead."

"You are right," Ed said, "There is nothing worse than when I found my bedside dresser drawer sprinkled with these. And the infestation I have noticed is also accompanied by an odor which what shall I say is kind of, 'roachy'.

"And, Ed," Rusty continued, "Remember when you pour grease down the drain, you're feeding the roaches so don't let that happen again."

Although Ed did not ask Rusty for a date because she was already married she gave him a tip to list a home in the Riverbend subdivision.

CHAPTER 7

That same evening Ed drove to the Riverbend subdivision where Rusty's friend Gillian, lived and upon approaching her home saw a sign on the lawn that read: "For Sale By Owner. Best Deal in Town" and underneath "Only $1,000."

Ed thought the price was a misprint but he called on Gillian just the same. Gillian, who appeared a bit distressed, showed him the 5000 square floor home which had a panoramic view of Edmonton and the Saskatchewan River that flowed through it.

While showing the swimming pool and the tennis court Gillian said, "You are the second person to show interest in my home."

Ed said the house and the landscaping was the most beautiful he had seen in Edmonton but leery about the $1,000 price when most homes in the area sold far above $500. 000.

"What's the catch?"

Gillian assured Ed that the mortgage and taxes were paid, "And there are no liens against it."

Ed was still leery about the price.

"Well, I'll be truthful," Gillian said, "Last week I got a call from my husband who informed me that he's leaving me for his secretary.

He then told me that I could have everything we owned as long as he could have the proceeds from the sale of the house. I agreed and asked if I could sell it quickly as I can while he and his lovey-dovey are spending their time in the Caribbean."

"I live in a condo and enjoy suburban living. If that is the case I'll buy your home and pay you its real value," Ed said.

Gillian's response was, "Ed, you are a bit late. The man ahead of you did. We are just waiting to have it conveyed.

"Congratulations! Then can I at least take you out for dinner?"

"Thank you for the invitation but the gentleman who bought the house, I already accepted his."

Next day Ed's father reminded his son, "Look, your deadline is fast approaching and your mother's health is deteriorating, why you don't try bungee jumping? I hear by the grapevine many young women have taken up the latest phenomena."

"Don't," his mother argued, "Bungee jumping can be dangerous. Why don't you go to the Equestrian Centre and while riding horses you may possibly meet a mate and fall in love."

Not to displease his parents Ed did both.

At the time bridges were beginning to replace telephone towers as a favored spot to practice jumping so Ed went to the High Level Bridge where there were other jumpers and had a fall of his life time. The jump gave Ed an adrenaline rush that only a near- death experience can provide.

Ed wasn't prepared to die yet so on his next day off he headed to the Equestrian Centre where he hoped to meet singles who were as horse loving as he was.

Ed chatted with Yvonne, who he thought was 'all-right' and got the latest equestrian news. He watched her make a practice run on Prince a four-year-old Quarter horse she was training for barrel racing.

Yvonne was an accomplished rider who competed since she was a child but as she and her horse rounded the third barrel, the animal slipped and fell. As Prince struggled to get up Yvonne's foot became trapped in the stirrup.

Startled, the gelding broke across the arena at a run, bucking and kicking. Everything seemed to move in slow motion as those present rushed into the arena to trap the horse. Suddenly, the horse kicked out, his hoof catching Yvonne in the middle of her back. The blow knocked her boot from the stirrup and Yvonne lay unconscious with blood streaming from beneath the helmet secured on her head.

Minutes passed an ambulance arrived. Following the trip to the University Of Alberta Hospital Yvonne used abusive language and became combative in the trauma room. Ed felt let down and did not see Yvonne again.

Ed did not sleep that night and during next and when he came home he felt tired and weary and needed 30 minutes of peace and quiet to unwind from the strains and stresses he had suffered. Unfortunately during that time Ed made several blunders including forgetting that he was potty trained and to pay his utility bills.

On the following night when Ed came home from work and in order to fall asleep faster exercised for thirty minutes, drank a glass of warm milk, a natural sleep enhancer, and then sat on his bed thinking what a traditional wedding would be like and who to invite.

Should the wedding be a grand event or a small gathering with close friends and family? What the brides wedding dress would be like? The color of the bridesmaid's dresses and of courses where the reception would take place and how much liquor to buy.

Who would do the catering and type of refreshments to serve? There was no doubt in Ed's mind that Reverend Taylor would perform the ceremony, although he wondered how much to tip him and who was going to pay for the wedding expenses. Then after thinking about his marriage, love and expenses Ed had a creative idea. At the appropriate time he would not depend on his parents but sell ads to corporate sponsors to pay for the wedding.

Still Ed wasn't feeling well so in the morning went to a 'no appointment necessary' clinic where following a physical the doctor on duty, Dr. Art Simpson, diagnosed Ed's condition as CRAFT disease.

"Craft disease?" What is it? I haven't heard of the disease. What are the symptoms?"\
"The symptom is that you can't remember a friggin thing. It's the first stage of dementia."

Ed wasn't the type of person who accepted jokes so he went to similar clinic on the next street and doctor on duty there, Henry Yutuc, following a physical examination twitched the ends of his mustache and said, "Sir, my diagnosis is that you have a slight case of what is commonly know as Furniture Disease."

Again Ed asked for the symptoms and was told, "Seems that your chest keeps falling into your drawers."

"This is no laughing matter," Ed thought. He was concerned about the state of his health. and made a swift exit to see his regular family doctor, Stan Hardy.

Once another physical examination was completed the doc sat next to Ed and confidentially said," Ed my friend, your other diagnoses is wrong. There is really nothing wrong with you that *Viagra* can not help."

Dr. Hardy wrote a prescription which Ed held in his hand and then purchased the sex enhancement pills at Shoppers Drug Mart.

Ed was excited thinking his down- feeling would disappear and hastily drove to his parent's home where upon showing the pills to his mother she got angry.

"At your age? You should be ashamed of yourself," she complained and flung the prescription bottle out the door which landed in a neighbor's back yard. There the chickens, believing the tablets were a food supplement, swallowed them one after another and the following day began laying hard boiled eggs.

By now Ed was tired of searching for someone that he could love, lean on, do his laundry and cook. He even had thoughts of remaining a bachelor for rest of his life until his condo neighbor, John, visited him and said, "Hey, Ed, why don't you try West Edmonton Mall which is the largest in North America and the 6th largest in the world and where all sorts of beautiful women shop and congregate?"

Ed listened eagerly and in the end said, "An excellent idea my friend!" And while jumping to his feet, a picture of Pamela Anderson fell off the living room wall facing him and shattered.

Then Ed said, to his condo neighbor, "I'm tired of kissing any more toads. Maybe you are right that I've been searching in the wrong places."

To find out on the following evening after work, Ed drove to West Edmonton Mall where he found a directory and then went to the Galaxy Amusement Park where he met up with Rose who rejuvenated him after both held their breath as they rode the Mindbender. They then laughed and screamed as they rode the world's largest indoor triple load roller coaster.

"I have heard WEM was a magical place," Ed thought and then invited Rose to ride a mechanical bull.

Ed rode first and when it was Rose's turn she climbed the animal and circled her hands over her head.

As Rose rode the mechanical bull he went wild beneath her, bucking her off before she knew her ride had begun. Poor Rose had injured her spleen and hasn't been seen or heard from since.

The following day a co-worker at Best Realty, Jack, said, "Why don't you take a holiday? I've been to Kelowna, British Columbia and it's a city where girls in bikinis stroll the beaches of Okanagan Lake. It's a city where I'd like to live when I retire."

Ed who was in a good mood went straight to *Everything Under the Sun* booking agency and as the clerk flew over a keyboard while humming *Love me Tender*, an Elvis Presley tune, she said, "An agenda for your holiday in Kelowna is completed." And handed it to him.

Ed took the first flight available to Kelowna where a *Welcome* billboard greeted him: "Kelowna – Population 125,000 and the home of Ogopogo who lives in Okanagan Lake."

During the first day of his vacation while Ed was lying on a sandy beach he met Courtney but she turned out to be a Creep so Ed said, "I'll pass."

On the second day however, Ed hooked up with curvaceous Louisa

He tasted Louisa's lips. No one had ever kissed him like this before. Not Trisha, Paulette, Alfa, not any of the predecessors. Louisa's kisses ignited deep into Ed's body shooting fireworks through every nerve ending.

Ed couldn't get enough of Louisa and thought he was in Heaven. As Ed was about to make a marriage proposal a not unusual thing for Kelowna happened. As the seagulls shrieked a violent thunder storm approached from the northeast. Okanagan Lake then had huge waves and whitecaps that began rolling. The waves were huge, really huge but not quite as huge as a tsunami.

Many years ago as the present, Indians in the Okanagan Valley would never paddle a canoe or a raft near the beach because often a storm would suddenly erupt and Ogopogo would surface and claim another life.

The Indians weren't superstitions and neither was Lisa.

Monsters, UFO's and the Sasquatch in general may have been an interesting topic for science fiction writers but seeing Ogopogo crawl out the water and approach the sunbathing couple, the torrid love affair ended quickly.

Louisa was about to give up her life as a human sacrifice while Ed fearing a thunderbolt may kill him rose to his feet, got his balance, put on his regular clothes and on departure said, "Good-bye, Louisa!"

Ed then hired a taxi which took him to the Kelowna Airport where he took a flight back home.

On his way back to Edmonton Ed stopped in Calgary one of the fastest growing communities in North America and used creative showmanship. Ed put on a Halloween costume, had a sandwich board spray painted that read: *Looking for Companionship – Possible Marriage*, with a phone number underneath and paraded in front of City Hall. Some critics called the innovative method of advertising, 'Crazy', 'Undignified' and 'Desperate' while women in front of City Hall cheered Ed on.

As soon as the one-hour parade was over Ed interviewed 14 ladies who were married and had left their husbands because they were abused in one way or another.
There were several singles too which included Begonia who was the most unlikely possible mate Ed had met and thought should have been arrested for terminal.
Ugliness.
Begonia was short and dumpy with one leg shorter than the other.
Seeing Begonia Ed almost passed out but had enough energy left to say, "I'll see you tomorrow."
But tomorrow never came and Ed felt her mother should have thrown her away and kept the stork.

Then there was Cynthia who excited Ed's senses. She was his height, had a small waist, very large blue eyes and auburn hair.
Her earrings where shaped like miniature hockey sticks and they sparkled as they dangled from her ear lobes to her chin. Cynthia wore a blue and red cowboy outfit with a ten gallon white hat. Ed and Cynthia hit it off and dated that evening.
Each enjoyed each others company and both liked the same things but Cynthia's topics of conversation seemed to be more important than Ed's.
After Ed and Cynthia met on the City Hall steps the couple then enjoyed delicious Western Canadian food to

eat and wine to drink at the restaurant on the top floor of the Calgary Tower. While enjoying the dinner and the panoramic view Ed and Cynthia exchanged smiles and aside from talking about the Calgary Stampede they compared notes about the Calgary Stampeder and Edmonton Eskimo football teams and then the Calgary Flames and Edmonton Oilers and their Battle of Alberta games.

Cynthia said that the Flames won a Stanley Cup and were a better team than the Oilers.

Well, Ed became agitated and replied, "Let's get the record straight. Oilers won five Stanley Cups. How can you say the Flames are a better team? That is why Edmonton is called City of Champions and Calgary Cow Town."

A disagreement erupted which city had the better hockey and football team and neither would give in. Their dating discontinued there on the top floor of the Calgary Tower.

Ed then made contact with the most saintly retired CBS newscaster/journalist icon in America, Walter Cronkite, in New York. Ed felt that since Cronkite helped many Americans during the Viet Nam war he could possibly perform a miracle and help him.

Unfortunately Cronkite wasn't canonized as saint yet neither was Peter Mansbridge of the CBC but Maxamillion (Ray) Kolbe of Poland was and when contacted suggested Ed ask hockey commentator Don Cherry for advice.

The following evening Ed discussed his search with icon Don Cherry of *Coach's Corner* during Hockey Night in Canada television fame. Since the legendary Cherry gave public tips about playing hockey and had a successful marriage, Ed figured the high-profile personality could also coach him in mate hunting.

Ed wasn't disappointed when Cherry advised, "Ed, be your own cheer leader, never cross check or take a slap-shot at a female, never change a winning lineup and do not be afraid to take your next prospective bride, any shape, fishing."

Ed took Cherry's advice seriously and met Nora in a lineup at Tim Horton's who was shaped like a Coca Cola bottle. After several dates Ed and Nora agreed to go fishing.

Without knowing why, they found themselves in Bonnyville whose motto is: "It's Multi-Natural" referring of course to its richness in natural gas and oil resources.

Of course if one lives in Edmonton, Vancouver or Toronto one may be tempted to call Bonnyville the largest cemetery in Alberta with shining lights.

But there are occasions that make the town come alive, especially when property owners receive their annual tax notices each spring, at election time and when the Indians block local roads frustrated because of unsettled land claims.

Although there is no Wal-Mart, Superstore, Canada Tire or Rona in the town there are many nearby lakes where tourists flock in order to catch the 'big' one. Ed and Nora registered at the Fishing Hole Motel at nearby Moose Lake.

Although it is said that birds do it, bees do it, even educated flees do it, not that Ed wasn't capable of doing it, nothing happened between Ed and Nora because the motel had a policy that required only twin beds.

And the beds had to be a minimum of two feet apart when a couple rented a room for only a week. At the same time it was illegal to make love on the floor between the beds.

It was a beautiful day in east-central Alberta and as soon as the two anglers registered they threw their lines into the lake and Nora hooked on to a Titanic jackfish that defies imagination. The fish was so huge that instead of Nora pulling it out; it bit her on the rear of her pants and pulled her into the lake. A struggle ensued and eventually Nora and the fish drifted into a stream, where there was a bridge on Highway 28.

Unfortunately Nora caught a corner by the seat of her pants. While the fish swam on its merry way Nora stayed suspended in the air until Ed rescued her an hour later and freed her from her misery.

You may not believe this but on the second day Ed and Nora went fishing again.

And when they launched their boat more fish were caught but then when a mosquito bit Nora she gave it a whack with her hand and in process lost her balance and fell into the lake.

Seeing Nora struggling those on the shore hollered, "Fish her out! Fish her out! Fish her out!"

But Ed still didn't know how to swim or even dive.

Several hours later Nora's body was found in ten meters of water. Ed was thunder struck as Nora was found at the bottom of the lake along with the hook, line and sinker – dead.

It wasn't the only time Ed dealt with death during his search for a mate. A week earlier at a time when Edmonton was becoming the Canadian motor vehicle fatality capital of Canada he added another to his list of perplexities while attending a Mom's Against Drunk Driving charity drive he met Sunday and Monday, twins born 11 minutes apart before and after midnight on a Sunday and a Monday, at the Royal Alexandra Hospital. They each weighed five pounds but Sunday was longer and remained taller as she grew.

Sunday and Monday were best of friends and always even as adults stuck together. They dressed in opposite colors of the same outfit, and insisted their hair be pinned exactly the same way and both were employed as cashiers at the Esso gas station and restaurant on Highway 16 at Androsson on the easterly outskirts of Edmonton.

Often the twins had arguments of course, but that did not matter, what did was Ed thought both were beautiful women and one could possibly be a mate as they had now reached 22 years of age.

On a typical Edmonton Friday evening Sunday got into her car, picked Monday up from work and were planning to go to an Edmonton casino for a night of fun and dancing.

At the intersection of 75th Street and Argyle Road on the way, Sunday was making a left hand turn when a pickup truck driven by a young man T-bared the car. The young man allegedly had stolen the vehicle and had been drinking.

Sunday and Monday were rushed by ambulance to the University of Alberta Hospital where both, like during their birth, died 11 minutes apart due to injuries received.

It was a month later that Ed was dating Sunday and Monday's older sister Emily who was employed as a cashier at Safeway in Edmonton. Emily accompanied Ed while driving to Vermilion to do a home estimate with the possibility of obtaining a listing.

While driving along Highway 16 and they reached the Esso Gas station and restaurant at Ardrosson Nancy unexpectedly said, "Ed, please stop. I see my sisters and want to speak to them."

Ed thought Nancy was a bit whacky and did not believe her twin sisters had come back to life. With a swift reaction Ed said, "But your sisters have died no more than a month ago."

"True but I like Martin Luther King had a dream. Mine was that the twins were alive and we would meet again to enjoy lunch at the Esso gas station restaurant where my sisters at one time were employed as cashiers."

Ed read metaphysical books and reincarnation made sense to him that the cyclical return of a soul came to another life in a new rebirth body.

Emily as a child attended the No Name Universal Church at Bible Study. As a teen she read metaphysical books and reincarnation made sense to her. She didn't speak openly about it at the time but it was her personal belief that she held for many years and continued to strive for greater knowledge and spiritual understanding.

After Sunday and Monday died the belief grew and grew breaking a hole in the sky recalling a psychic memory that she could recall in detail.

To make her belief more forceful Nancy said, "But I like you believe in reincarnation despite what theologians think is untrue."

Ed was concerned and said, "But I have read that if reincarnation takes place there has to be a crisis on the

Planet Earth and when one dies and is born again it's as a child and not an adult."

Emily's dream was triggered by a past memory supported by a hypnosis aggression that she had experienced earlier in life.

Ed pulled over to a curb and Nancy jumped out of Ed's Buick Regal and headed as fast as her legs could carry her to meet Sunday and Monday who to her were seen waiting at the restaurant entrance door.

For the next week Ed was in a state of grief and perplexity. Fearing further rejections he had thoughts of living with a robot instead a female.

A robot would not hurt his feelings nor argue like some housewives do, when his mother phoned and said, "Ed, my health is progressively getting worse.

Today I had an x-ray taken and my heart which is deteriorating and I have a high blood pressure. It now beats much faster than usual and it may soon explode," And continued: "Look, Bill Gates at Microsoft has come up with Window XP software for the personal computer that is selling like hot cakes. A computer dating service has just opened on Jasper Avenue. Why don't you go there for assistance?"

Ed accepted the suggestion as he was intrigued how this latest Microsoft Window software could add spice to his social life. Thirty dollars to open an account didn't seem expensive for three printouts. Ed was curious about the criteria the dating service used to match people.

Ed wanted to find out for instance, how this man/woman scheme worked so he polished his conversation skills and arranged an interview with Personal Dating Service where he filled out detailed evaluation test that included sections on general experience, religion, attitude towards sex, personal interests, a description of himself and a section on reaction situations.

With questions as thorough as these it seemed impossible not meet the ideal mate but it didn't work out that way. Ed dated three different dates from the computer printout, none of them he knew.

There was Helen who was a monster from *Star Wars*, Bamby from *Disneyland* who advised Ed against reading *Playboy* alleging the magazine was full of 'unpleasant subjects,' and Judy from an *Encounter of a Different Kind* who said her birthday was February 2nd. Well, she did look a bit like a groundhog.

Each was an emotional basket case.

Ed ordered three more printouts and again didn't know of any of the women. In the end he hoped it would remain that way. The six printouts generally were unintelligent, uninteresting and above all did not enjoy Country and Western music or current events.

Agnes was so bubbly and big-chested that when Ed went jogging with her there were seismic vibrations that could be felt a mile distant.

The second, Nichole, he could not put his heart on the line because she was a parasite for sore eyes and had so much plastic surgery done that her face looked like the Bad Land near Drumheller.

The third, Alfreda, reminded Ed of a Wood Buffalo Park whooping crane casualty hopping with a broken wing. Alfreda in Ed's opinion although beautiful, ambitions and restless was also cold, paranoid and neurotic.

On a scale of 1 to 10 most of the dates rated fewer than 4
and collectively Ed felt their
I Q didn't add up to the minimum wage paid in Alberta
at the time.

And Ashley's I. Q. wasn't much higher when she stayed
at Ed's condo while he had gone to Africa to seek a new
market. Ashley was opening the door as she was going
to work at the TD Canada Trust Bank and her key broke
off in the lock. After resorting in vain to screwdrivers
and pliers Ashley decided to call a locksmith who arrived
promptly and as she was looking through the peephole
said to him, "My key broke off inside the lock."
"On the inside? It will take at least an hour and I'll have
to charge you fifty dollars."
"I don't have that kind of money in Ed's condo right now
but as soon as I get out, I'll go to the bank and pay you."
"I'm sorry mam," the locksmith said." The locksmith
articulated with instructive courtesy, "I'm afraid as a
charter member of the Edmonton Locksmith's Union and
one who helped draw up the Collective Agreement I'm
prohibited from unlocking your door unless I'm paid in
advance."
"You're joking of course," Ashley said.
"The subject of the Locksmith's Union is no joking
manner. In drawing up the Collective Agreement no detail
has been overlooked and clause number 7 says, 'Gold shall
open doors and the doors shall adore it'."
"Please," Ashley pleaded. "Be reasonable. Open the door
for me and since I have no cash on hand I'll use my credit
card."
"I'm sorry. Our company doesn't accept credit cards
and further more there are ethics involved. Have a good
day."

Bewildered Ashley called the bank where she worked and informed her supervisor that she probably wouldn't be able to come to work that day and called another locksmith, and just in case, said to herself, "I'm not going to say I have no money until after he opens the door for me."

She searched the Yellow Pages directory and dialed a number'

"What address?" a guarded receptionist asked.

"XXX Jasper Avenue condo number 1201."

The receptionist hesitated and asked Ashley to repeat the address and when she did the receptionist said, "The place from where you are calling from is occupied by Ed Remus?"

"It is."

"Impossible. The Edmonton Locksmith's Union prohibits us from doing any work at that address."

Before another word was said the receptionist hung up.

Ashley went to Yellow Pages again and made a dozen phone calls to other locksmiths and the instant they heard the address and the mention of Ed Remus, they all refused to do the job.

To find a solution elsewhere Ashley called the condo manager and he replied, "In the first place, I don't know how to open locks, and in the second place, even if I did know, I wouldn't do it, since my job is taking care of the place and not letting suspicious birds out of their cages."

Ashley then called the bank where she worked in hopes that her supervisor could come and open the door.

"Bad luck," the supervisor said. "So you can't get out of your condo. You just never run out of excuses not to come to work."

At this point Ashley had a homicidal urge. She hung up, called the bank again and asked for a co-worker, Noel, that she knew well and a bit brighter than her supervisor.

Sure enough Noel seemed interested in finding a solution, "Tell me, was it the key or the lock that broke?"

"The key. Half of it is inside the lock. The doorknob won't work left or right."

"Why don't you don't try to get the piece that's stuck inside out with a set of pliers or a screw driver?"

"I tried both but it's impossible."

"Then you'll have to call a locksmith."

"I already have but they want a payment in advance."

"So pay them and there you are."

"But don't you understand. I have no money with me."

"You sure do have problems," Noel said and hung up.

And so ended the morning but in the afternoon Ashley began making more phone calls. But something she found frequent the telephone was out of order. Problem: how to request repair service without a telephone to place a call? She went to the 12th story balcony and began shouting at people walking along the sidewalk below.

The street noise was deafening. At most, an occasional person would raise their head distractedly and then continue.

Next she placed sheets of paper and carbons in the typewriter and composed the following message, "Madam or Sir: My key has broken off in the lock and I'm locked inside condo unit 1201. If you find this, please help me!" Ashley made the sheets of paper into little airplanes and threw them over the balcony railing and they fluttered a long time.

Some with the help of the wind flew as far as the Southgate Shopping Mall, some were run over by non-stop vehicles, some landed on awnings and other buildings but one dripped on a sidewalk where a diminutive gentleman picked it up and read it. He then looked up the balcony shading his eyes with his left hand. Ashley put on a friendly smile but the gentleman tore up the paper into many little pieces and with an irate gesture gave her the finger and hurled the pieces into the gutter.

Seconds turned to minutes and minutes turned into hours but even when it was beginning to get dark outside she continued throwing airplane messages from the balcony but they weren't either read, or if they were, weren't taken seriously. By late evening an envelope was slipped under Ed's condo door.

The telephone company cut of his service for non-payment. Then in succession they cut of his natural gas, electricity and water and that's when Ashley got angry and with her fists continuously banged on the door causing noise that reverberated throughout the 12th condo floor.

When Ed's business conference ended he did some sight-seeing before his flight home.

At the end Ed discovered the small town offered no taxi or bus to the airport. Desperate, Ed called a parcel delivery service and asked what it would cost to send a parcel to the airport.

"Five dollars, sir."

"Does it matter how large the parcel?"

"So long it fits into the delivery truck."

Ed climbed into a large package container.

A short while later the congenial deliveryman picked up his 'parcel' and got Ed to the airport on time.

As soon as Ed returned from doing business in Africa he paid his power, gas, telephone and locksmith bills. As soon as the door was opened Ed erased Ashley's name as a possible lifetime mate. But not before she asked, "Ed, what did you miss most while in Africa?"

Ed paused and then said, "Toilet paper."

It was goodbye to Ashley and next day while picking up a parcel at the Greyhound Bus Depot Ed met Liz who had purchased bus fare to Winnipeg at a time the crime rate in Edmonton experienced another homicide. There was no dating however because Ed discovered like Lizzy Borden in Massachusetts this Liz had taken a hatchet and gave her mother 40 whacks and then when this was done she gave her father another 41.

Minutes later the mystery why Liz committed a homicide reached its climax when this beautiful woman was charged with slaying her parents. According to police the murders weren't done for pleasure or spite but because Liz wasn't very bright.

Ed then hooked up with Tiffany, a gorgeous single parent and a bit older than Ed, who tended to talk to herself and had a sense of humour. Tiffany took care not to resort to insults and teasing. Her quirks, faults and habits however at times could be annoying and her actions were always environment friendly. During each date Ed and Tiffany would attend comedy movies and enjoyed watching *Air Farce*. The Red Green Show and *Just for Laughs* on television and struck with awe the antics of comics Rick Mercer, Cathy Jones and Ron James.

"Humour seems to run in our family. My son is always wisecracking and my sister Ping has a wonderful sense of ridiculousness," Tiffany said and continued, "I, like you Ed, haven't exactly sailed through life on a sea of belly laughs."

Tiffany was a keen observer of life and had her share of illness, heartache and tragedy.

However, her comic vision survived particularly during shorter and colder days. As Tiffany was dedicated to help the poor by volunteering as a coordinator at the Inn Roads Housing Co-operative on Boyle Street. Ed because of selling real estate and had a deadline to meet and Tiffany because of her commitment to volunteer work, dated only for a short while but remained friends.

CHAPTER 8

Several days later associate realtor Adam took Ed aside and said, "Look, facing a relationship is a challenge, you are still single, alone, have a deadline to meet and struggling to find the ideal mate. Stop struggling and moping. I have some advice for you which will expedite the process. I ordered a mail order bride from Russia although my marriage failed, yours may not."

Adam then handed Ed an International Mail Order Bride catalogue with photos of beautiful women who were disenchanted with the Russian dating scene.

The idea of mail order brides was around since the early settlers, would write back to their homeland for a bride and the term "Mail-Order-Brides" was born. But before Ed would order a potential bride and receive one in the mail, he nosed about and found why Adam's marriage had failed.

Nataliya was a 26-year-old college student when she met Adam a handsome, successful Edmonton businessman. They met in Moscow. Love however, did not conquer all. At first Nataliya and Adam were happy in their married life but two months later Adam began abusing her physically. One night he beat her at the time she was breast feeding the couple's infant daughter. Nataliya wound up in the Royal Alexandra Hospital emergency room with her face bruised and swollen and a human bite mark on her hand.

Once released from the hospital Nataliya escaped to a woman's shelter, then got a radical and sued the International Mail Order agency for not screening Adam properly.

Ed felt that in obtaining a mail-order-bride there would be a language barrier and also it was a time that Ed's credit card had had reached its limit.

One failure to meet the appropriate mate led to another. It wasn't because lack of effort however, as Ed did everything possible in a fast paced environment that his parents told him to do. But no matter how hard he worked or how much effort he put in, none seemed to work.

A day later while shopping at West Edmonton Mall Ed had a conversation with Shirley but since he was focused on learning how to swim at the Fantasy Land Hotel pool that day he put dating her on the back-burner. Ed knew however, it was time to burn another bridge so the following evening he phoned Shirley that at first tried her hand at being a model but ended up as a merchandiser at Wal-Mart and she excitedly replied, " Hey good looking, what's cooking? I'm free and ready to go steady but don't tell your mother."

Ed and Shirley fell madly in love but before Ed would get engaged he called his mother to share the good news and arranged for the couple to have dinner with his parents so they could meet his fiancé.

To Ed Shirley was stunningly beautiful with blue eyes with a tattoo on her body and a ring in her nose. She was wearing a loose floral mini dress with shoulder straps. Her red hair was done porcupine style. Shirley liked to dance, mainly hip-hop and also enjoyed singing the latest rap songs.

After the sumptuous dinner was eaten Ed took his mother aside and in their privacy asked, "Well, Mom, what you think of Shirley as your prospective daughter in-law?" Shirley was exactly the sort Ed's mother objected to and coldly replied, "She's a queer one. I can't stand her." And the following day when Ed introduced Shirley to his employer, George Best, Best replied, "Ed, if you marry her you'll have to find yourself a new employer."

Since Ed sensed there would be unhappiness between his mother and his wife he disposed Shirley and hooked up with Ivy who with her aging mother Roberta, which he didn't particularly like, accompanied the couple on a short vacation to the Middle East to visit their relatives. During the vacation while visiting Jerusalem Ivy's mother died. Coming out of one crises Ed headed for another when with a death certificate in hand he went to the Canadian Consulate Office to help Ivy make arrangements to send the body back to Edmonton for burial.

The Consul, after hearing of the death of Ed's possible mother-in-law, said to Ed, "My friend, to bring the body back to Edmonton for burial is very expensive and could cost as much as $10,000."
The Consul continued by saying, "In most cases the person responsible for the remains normally buries the body here. This would only cost $5000."
Ed thought for a moment and then replied, "I don't care how much it will cost to send the remains back to Edmonton. That's what Ivy wants to do."
After hearing about the death in more detail the Consul said, "You must have loved your future mother-in-law very much considering the difference in price between $10,000 and $5, 000."

"It's not that," Ed said, feeling uncomfortable. "You see, I know of a case many, many years ago of a person that was buried in Jerusalem, and on the third day he was resurrected. Consequently, I don't want to take that chance with my prospective mother-in-law."

When Ed and Ivy returned to Edmonton Ivy the dynamics of the couple was shaky. Humiliated by Ed's attitude toward her mother Ed and Ivy did not date again.

As the trip from Jerusalem to Edmonton was exhausting and Ed still suffering from jetlag he slept what he felt was a day and a night. It really was 30 minutes by his watch when he received a phone call from Dr. Hardy who softly said, "Ed my friend, I have some bad news and some good news for you. Which do you want to hear first?"

"The bad news," Ed said.

"The bad news is that your mother has just died."

"Oh, no!" And I haven't met my deadline. What is the good news?"

The good news is that the doctors at the University Of Alberta Hospital have used a laser and hypnosis and they brought her back to life."

"Mom has been revitalized?"

"And in good health but keep on searching because your mother may have a relapse."

Relieved, Ed thought one way for finding a mate and lead a contented life was to date Elvira who was a vegetarian and her physical attractiveness wasn't a pinnacle for a relationship. After several dates Elvira prepared Ed a large bowl of vegetable soup but he had a yearning for a meal that had meat and potatoes as part of a diet.

Next day stopped at the nearby Aboriginal Restaurant where a Native lady, Betty Cardinal, served him a fine meal consisting of meat and potatoes.

Since Ed hadn't eaten meat for some time he complimented Betty for a tasty meal she had served him.

"This is the best meal I had in a long time. It was kind of delicious but what kind of meat did you use?" he asked.

"Moose meat," Betty replied,

Moose meat and potatoes seemed to settle Ed's stomach but he preferred to eat Alberta beef rather than wild meat so any romance between him and Elvira and Betty did not take place.

Ed then hooked up with Edna (No relation to Dame Edna), a member of the Edmonton based military 1st Battalion, Princess Patricia's Light Infantry. The relationship between Ed and the beautiful Edna did not last long however. After several dates Edna along with 2,200 other Canadian soldiers was assigned to Afghanistan to democratize the country and fight the insurgent Taliban and their support of al Qaeda terrorists.

Ed had mixed feelings about the war in Afghanistan but Edna was itching to help her comrades and said, "This is why I joined. Everyone knows there will be Taliban attacks and if a Canadian solider should get killed there will be stress at the Edmonton Garrison. Ed stole a minute and after a quick hug said, "Edna, I hope your heart feels no pain and I hasten to bid you adieu but please remember that I will miss you."

A store that helps men find a true love just opened in a tall building in Edmonton. Among the instructions at the entrance is a description how the store operates. You may visit the store Only Once. There are six floors and the attributes of the women increase as the shopper ascends the flights.

There was however, a catch: one could choose any woman from a particular floor, or may choose to go up a floor. But you cannot go back down except to exit the building.

So on a day that Ed was frustrated with his search and thought life was made up of love and work, and love came first, he went to the Women Store to find a mate. On the first floor the sign on the door read: These lovely women are employed. The second floor sign reads: These women are employed and love children. The third floor sign reads: These women are employed, love children and are extremely good looking.

Ed thought, "Wow!" But felt compelled to keep going so he went to the 4th floor and the sign read: These women are employed, love children, are good living and are exceptional cooks.

"Oh, mercy me!" Ed exclaimed. "I can hardly stand it!" Still he went to the 5th floor where the sign read: These women are employed, love children, are gorgeous looking, help with housework and have a strong romantic streak'.

Ed was temped to stay but went to the 6th floor and the sign read: 'You are visitor 32,456, to this floor. There are no women here. This floor exists only as proof that men are impossible to please. Thank you for shopping at the Women Store.

Being left alone Ed then had an idea. "There are same-sex marriages taking place throughout Canada and California so why can't I marry myself?"

Ed had just spent time studying the Bible in excruciating detail and noticed that Leviticus warned Christians not marry their sister, aunt, mother, mother-in-law, daughter or even their granddaughter (should they be tempted). But nowhere in the good book was there a rule against marrying oneself.

Of course the *Bible* also neglects to forbid anyone from marrying great-grandmothers, a budgie bird, or a pet fish. Although his parents were against self-marriages it was Reverend Taylor who slept with a French poodle that said, "Why not?"

When Reverend Taylor recited the marriage vows he said, "Ed Remus, will you promise yourself as a husband also to be your own wife, to live as one in marriage? Will you love and comfort yourself, obey and honor yourself in sickness and in health and be faithful and honor yourself as long as you shall live?"

"I do," Ed said.

Ed had reasons for marrying himself when he did. Ever since he knew the concept of wedlock, he longed for a partner he could trust and could tell his deepest secrets without his parents knowing them.

Altogether Ed thought his marriage was a success for most part. He rarely argued with himself. In a few times that he did he always won. And as far as sex went, well it was whatever he made of it.

After a week of solitary married life Ed's sales weren't going that well so he decided to split but Pastor Taylor said he couldn't just file for a divorce on a moments notice, he had to have legitimate justification. Wanting to have a baby wasn't on the list of good reasons to divorce.

As the Reverend explained, Ed could only divorce if he had been living apart from his spouse for at least a year which would be difficult without major surgery or if his spouse had been treated with cruelty or imprisoned.

Ed wasn't particularly willing to beat himself up or lounge around in prison so he could divorce himself. That left one option—adultery.

Ed got legal advice from one of Edmonton leading attorneys, Thomas Huff, who was so caught up in his work that he didn't have time to publish his dream book titled *Making Divorce Work in Five Easy Steps.*

It was a common saying in Edmonton that if one got into the rough to consult with Huff.

who had 25 years experience on divorce matters and advised Ed that he did not necessarily have to have sex with someone in order to get a divorce.

Upon that advice Ed removed his wedding ring and since the divorce was an amicable one, he divorced himself without paying a huge lawyer's fee and became single again.

Ed went away whistling from Huff's office but the yearning for a female mate continued. The following day while still dreaming of the woman who would become his mate Ed purchased a laptop computer to speed up his search. He then subscribed to the internet and with Google assistance clicked on the website *Find a Mate* chatting room.

Ed first chatted with Reba in Houston, Texas and things went fine until she sent her internet photo as an attachment and Ed discovered Houston was the number one obese city in America. With Reba car was king, the drive-through the rule and diabetes 2 began in many cases at age eight. Most of Reba's activities centered watching television, surfing the net, video games and on texting the phone. When 23-year-old Reba said she weighed 331 pounds, her sister 360 and 12-year-old brother 327, that did it. Ed and Reba did not chat again.

The following day Ed connected with Angelfish right from the start.

Angelfish (whose real name was Nina), and employed by Service Canada in Saskatoon, Saskatchewan. Angelfish seemed like a genuine single after she bought herself a cellular phone so they could text each other.

Ed and Angelfish never ran out of things to say to each other. They got to meet in person after Angelfish jetted from Saskatoon and Ed picked her up at the International airport. As they drove throughout the city there was lot of loving and kissing as she twirled Ed's hair in her fingers. This continued during dinner that night at the romantic The Creperie Restaurant. Ed was pleasantly surprised with Angelfish's appearance and demeanor where they giggled as if they were already married.

"Angelfish has a huge soul and when she laughs the sun comes out," Ed thought.

On the third day however, Ed scolded his potential bride for wasting a roll of colored wrapping paper imported from China. (Everything seemed to be imported from China at the time).

Ed became infuriated when Angelfish tried to decorate a box to give him as a birthday present. Never the less Angelfish brought the gift to Ed and said, "This is for you Ed, Happy Birthday."

Ed was embarrassed by his earlier overreaction but his anger flared again when he found the box was empty. Ed yelled at Angelfish, "Don't you know when you give someone a present, there is supposed to be something inside?"

Angelfish looked at Ed pensively and said, "Ed, it's not empty at all. I blew kisses into the box. They are for you, my love."

Ed was crushed. He put his arms around Angelfish and asked for forgiveness. Only during the same day Angelfish received word from her supervisor that she was promoted and to start working in Ottawa.

Ed kept that gold colored box by his bedside however, and when ever he was discouraged, he would take out an imaginary kiss and remember the love Angelfish gave him.

Ed was beginning to feel that he would never find the appropriate mate until he met with psychic Madame Tikova, a romance specialist who recently published a book entitled *One Step to Finding a Mate and Lead a Contented Life*. Her success in finding someone special was well documented using a combination of: "Instinct personality, profiling and science."

While fingering her programmed Blackberry Madam Tikova continued, "Alas, there's someone out there for everybody. In fact there are a lot of someone's out there. It has nothing to do with going to bars, cooking contests, rock climbing, shopping, fishing or playing golf together. The problem is that too often people search for their –life-long partner through clubs, organization and suggestions by their parents not suited to their personalities, culture, lifestyle and they seldom make the grade because of mistakes they make. Ed, this is a reason why so many blind dates arranged by well-intentioned friends and family tend to bomb, and why so many

seemingly perfect marriages end up abruptly in divorce."
"What kind of mistakes?"
"Well, let's take males for example. Males talk too much
about past dates and themselves and they try too hard to
impress females."
"How about females?"
"Females mentally march every man they date up the
aisle, they tend to burst into tears, dress inappropriately
and trash their ex-boyfriends and husbands."
Madame Tikova next pulled out from her desk drawer a
sheet of paper and said, "Here are names of two women:
Faith and Hope which I have short listed. Why don't you
date one of them and see how you make out."

These were heady times for Ed and as the search raced on
he said, "Let's do that," and his first date was with Faith
who suffered from, "What ever" and a fitness freak. After
watching her body language and listening to her love-
gone-wrong talk Ed noticed that Faith was communicating
with the spirits of John Lennon the former Beatle and then
the late Princes Diana.
Although Ed believed there was real estate on the Moon
he did not believe one could séance with the dead.
And then when Faith said, "When I got up this morning,
I took two Ex-Lax tablets in addition to my Prozac."
That did it and any possible romance with Faith did not
take place.

Undeterred, Ed's hopes and vision of being married were
fading so next he dated Hope who was trying to find a
man willing to become an instant father for her three year
old son, Mike.
Ed didn't want a relationship where he would have to take
care of one's baggage or a woman who was a member

of the *Alien Gospel* sect that had taboos about almost everything including the avoidance of eating red meat but beans instead.

To eat only beans one had to fart which would disturb Ed's concentration and keep clients away so the couple split and there was no romance with Hope.

By now Ed was nearly a year older, a little smarter and prayed more often so when things were going wrong as most of the time they did, and the road Ed was trudging was uphill, funds were getting low and debts getting higher Ed took on as his personal motto: "Everything comes to him who waits."

Ed realized that at the same time he had a deadline to meet and if he was patient and energetic he would eventually succeed in finding a compatible mate and marry her. Upon a suggestion of his mother Ed went to see the ultimate local health healer, Nana Bijou who had a Ph D and specialized in angel therapy. The elderly Mrs. Bijou was a religious person with thirty years experience in spiritual healing. Ed's mother said Mrs. Bijou had a special gift of healing in a unique way that makes one feel good about themselves. Neighbors however called her, "The Old Witch with magic power."

When Ed met the elderly Mrs. Bijou at her home it was near midnight but she was still energetic and bubbly with an intuitive sense of knowing how frustrated Ed was. Because Mrs. Bijou loved to inspire people in order to fulfill their dreams she placed her hands on both sides of Ed's head and whispered several sentences. She then asked Ed to take her hand and pray with her in saying the, "Lord's Prayer."

This done Mrs. Bijou said, "Ed, may God bless you. Tomorrow a guardian angel will deliver your ever-loving mate to Churchill Square at approximately 12:30."

"Really? I'll wait at the footsteps of the City Hall," Ed replied then after giving the faith healer a hug said, "I'll anxiously wait and thank God for the part you played."

"A promise is a promise. It's getting late so go home and rest," Mrs. Bijou replied

The following June afternoon there wasn't a cloud in the sky. It was windless and sunny with fresh warmth of a summer day. The flowers in Churchill Square in front of City Hall and next to the City Centre Mall were blossoming profusely as Archangel Michael flew over Edmonton and circled the square before landing. At the same time a trumpet sounded as if at the last judgment. After landing in the square and hundreds of onlookers, including friends and relatives watching, the angel introduced Charity Cane to Ed Remus and the couple embraced each other. To this point in time Ed had met many great women but none as great as Charity. Turning to Archangel Michael Ed said, "Thank you my dearest angel. I was delivered what I prayed for into the arms I was made for. Thank you for delivering Charity to me. Dearest angel I went through a daily struggle but now feel blessed and oh so lucky."

Then addressing his true love, Charity, Ed continued, "With love that is true you are worth waiting for. I now caress you and want to press you to my heart."

Within one-hour archangel Michael returned to Heaven. Charity had returned to her parents' farm near Saint Albert after she had received her diploma in husbandry at the Olds College of Agriculture. Her parents did not sell their farm because they were able to obtain a low interest

Credit Union loan to purchase enough fertilizer which they were unable the year before at a bank.

Following a short courtship Ed found that he and Charity had the same astrophysical sign. He found Charity attractive, kind, honest, and her imagination fertile.
Both enjoyed Country and Western music, reading newspapers and watching television about the war in Iraq and Canadian forces in Afghanistan and the upcoming federal election. Above anything else Charity liked Ed's personality.

On the minus side Charity at times appeared insecure. That insecurity eventually disappeared after she invited Ed and his parents to a farm barbecue where Ed fell off a horse, was chased by a bull, bit by a dog and in the event Ed needed another career, was taught how to properly milk a cow.

The barbecue was a great success because that evening there was a happy event after Ed said, "Charity, you are adorable," and Charity responded with, "And so are you Ed. I think you are sweet. I feel as if I had known you for a long time. It's great the way you make me feel."
Ed's heart began to flutter as he got on his knees and taking Charity by her arm, asked her to close her eyes and after saying, "No peeking", continued, "Charity, will you marry me?"
Charity unhesitatingly replied, "Oh dear, I kept your calling card close to my heart and soul. I thought you'd never ask. Ed you are patient and loving. I don't think I could ask for anything more. I would be delighted to be Mrs. Remus for the rest of my life and longer. I'm a victim

of your charms and letting the world know that I'm yours forever."

Ed had gone through many storms. Finally satisfied his mate expectations had been met and as triumph had been reached over adversity, he slipped an engagement ring on Charity's finger and finally convinced his parents that he could find a bride within one year.

Minutes later Charity and Ed, there inside the barn, among the hay, flies buzzing, hens clucking and roosters crowing agreed to a traditional marriage.

This done, Charity and Ed promised to love each other until they had to have false teeth and announced their wedding date as the following August..

As soon as Charity changed her status from being a country single girl to Ed's fiancé Ed never had been happier now that he had found a loving life-long mate which met his expectations. Ed's parents and those who knew Ed were relieved. Ed and Charity were happy too as parents' from both sides promised to help with the wedding arrangements.

ED AND CHARITY'S WEDDING

CHAPTER 9

No event in Edmonton, not the Queen's visit or even the Oilers winning the Stanley or the Eskimos the Grey Cups was more exciting than Ed and Charity's wedding, arranged for the third Saturday of August 2008. By now Ed and Charity had paid for their $24,000 wedding by selling advertising space at the ceremony and reception. Everything from the wedding rings to a week at the Fairmont Banff Springs Hotel was donated after Ed and Charity got 24 companies to sponsor the nuptials in exchange of having their names appear on the invitations to the thank-you cards. Ed did cough up his own money for his wife's $1500 engagement ring while Charity paid $1000 for her wedding dress.

The *Sun* ran a photo of the couple sitting among their corporate sponsored wedding "gifts" in its Sunday edition. Charity however drew the line by not having advertising banners draped across the church aisle but not at the reception. But her perfume came from *Spasation Salon and Spa*. Coffee was provided gratis by *Tim Horton's*. Advertisers had their names appear on the invitation and thank-you cards, napkins at the dinner table and in an ad placed in the Sun newspaper.

Ed woke before dawn and at 9:00 he and his best man, close friend by the name of Adam, went to pick up their tuxedos' that had been booked six weeks earlier but no one had placed the order. The only thing *Formalwear Rental Shop* could come up with was winter suits and there were no shoes to match. The expected temperature in Edmonton was forecast to be 31C degrees. As Ed left the store he placed the bag containing the suits on top of his Buick Regal and drove away. The bag, besides containing the winter suits also contained Ed's wallet which contained money to pay for the use of the Westmount Community hall and the bridle suite in the Fairmont Macdonald Hotel in Edmonton, the liquor license for the reception and all his credit and identification cards. Realizing his loss Ed drove back to the store but couldn't find the bag so he called police and *Visa*

Charity's day was going just as badly as she couldn't decide if her toenails should be red or blue. And at the *His and Her Salon* Charity's bridesmaids turned shades of white and green and then after eating at the Oriental Noodle House, Charity herself asked the waitress, "Where is the washroom? Quickly because I'm going to throw up."

As the marriage hours were approaching the comedy of errors continued. Charity had difficulty wakening before she had to leave for the No Name Universal Reformed Church.
Meanwhile at Ed's wedding group Ed, the best man and Charity's brother were enjoying a glass of his home-

brewed beer and decorating the car with crepe paper and flowers.

As the three men were decorating police called and said they had found the lost bag. It was 1:00 p. m. and the wedding was to begin at 3:00.

Police asked Ed to pick up the bag and wallet before 2:00.

Fortunately Ed picked up the bag and wallet on time but on his way back 95% of the flowers decorating the car had blown away by a gust of wind. Then on his way to the church his car had a flat tire. The rim was rusted so badly that the tire couldn't be taken off.

Ed ended up leaving the car where it was while he and the best man rushed to the nearest service station to purchase a can of rust remover. When Ed returned to the car there was a traffic violation ticket with a note attached on the windshield which read, "Hope your wedding ceremony goes better than your car."

It didn't.

As the No Name Universal Church bells were ringing and the birds singing their loudest. The wedding ceremony was an hour late not because of Ed's doing but because bees were out in full force that day and Charity had one stuck in her veil and her mother had difficulty to dig it out.

Then while entering the church with her father Charity was wearing a white dress and veil and carrying a bouquet of flowers. At the same time the organist was playing and the Full Gospel Choir singing the traditional, *Here Comes the Bride*. All of a sudden Charity tripped and fell. When she picked herself up and continued walking down the aisle someone pushed the organist aside and began playing, *"The Lady is a Tramp"*

Charity was still in the arms of her father who as he was handing his daughter to the restless Ed, Charity paused, kissed her father and then whispered, "Dad, we do not want underwear for Christmas this year. Just give us your credit card."

Those near the front pews responded with ripples of laughter and even the minister smiled broadly.

Then as the bride and groom walked forward Ed stepped on her train snapping the elastic. Once the elastic was retrieved Ed and Charity walked together until they reached the altar where they realized Reverend Taylor wasn't marrying them but a novice substitute female minister from Lac La Biche. Reverend Taylor was taken ill after a noodle at the Oriental Noodle House had stuck in his larynx and the doctor attending him said, "You must not preach for at least another week."

The marriage ceremony was going on without a glitch until blessing of the ring and the substitute minister waved her hand and the elastic in Charity's veil gave way flying ten feet behind her. The minister then covered the microphone in front of her with her hand and to the bride and groom said softly, "That was a powerful blessing, wasn't it?"

Then when the minister came to the part, "If anyone has reason why these two people should not marry, speak up now or forever hold your peace," a boy about five years of age, ran up the aisle yelling, "Daddy, Daddy, I'm here!"

The joke, planned by the best man, aroused the crowd that it took five minutes before the Gospel Choir sang *Bringing In The Sheaves* and the ceremony continued.

When it was time for vow-taking the minister said, "A circle is the symbol of the sun and the earth and the universe, of wholeness and perfection, and peace and love. It is worn on the third finger because of an ancient Greek belief that a vein from that finger goes directly to the heart.

"These rings mark the beginning of a long journey together. Wear them proudly, for they are symbols which speak of the love that you have for each other."

The wedding vows are the words how much the bride and groom love each other. To express exactly how Ed and Charity felt their creative juices were flowing when they wrote their own vows earlier for the joyous occasion.

Turning towards Ed she continued, "And do you Ed Remus, promise that when you go shopping at West Edmonton Mall that you will not get lost?"

"I do."

And do you Candy Cane promise that when you are out publicly with Ed you will not eat garlic, onions or sardines and not forget to brush your teeth?"

"I do but my name isn't Candy, its Charity."

Ed and Charity beamed after the minister married the couple by saying, "Charity Cane, Ed Remus's peach and Ed Remus, Charity Cane's plum, I now pronounce you a fruit salad."

The substitute minister did not use the conventional, 'For better or worse until death do us part', because it wasn't fashionable in Edmonton to be married for a life time – four years the most and then a divorce. And there was a movement throughout Canada to have same-sex marriages accepted as an individual's right.

Later in the ceremony as the minister was about to preach about bonds and unity Ed and Charity could not light the unity candle because the wick hadn't been straightened out. After a full minute of holding their candles over the unity one with no results, the minister pulled out a pocket knife from her pocket and dug the wick out to everyone's relief.

But due to the smell from the perfumed burning wax and no air conditioning Ed's mother began swaying back and forth and then passed out.

After the one-hour ceremony of vow-taking and signing the register the organist played and the Gospel Choir sang as part of the recessional ceremony, the Realtor's hyme *I Got a Mission Just Over the Hilltop.* Ed and Charity then emerged arm-in arm in front of the church to the delight of the wedding guests and other onlookers, who blew soap bubbles at the bride and groom. Why soap bubble instead of rice? Because according to Charity who knew something about agriculture, there was a shortage of rice for dinner plates in Thailand and the Philippines.

A short time later the bride and groom disappeared and after formal portraits were taken, the best man drove the couple to the Westmount Community Hall where the reception was held and its inside walls decorated with flowers, balloons, candles and a papered heart banner sign hanging from the ceiling that read: *The Following Sponsors Wish Charity and Ed Life-Time Happiness.* Underneath in smaller print were the names of the 24 sponsors that included: Best Realty, Epcor, Telus, City Centre Mall, Noodle Noodle Chinese Restaurant, Tim Horton's, Fairmont MacDonald Hotel, Café Supreme, KFC, Italian Bakery, West Jet Airline, UFA, Shaw Cable, Safeway, Home Depot, Staples. COLD-FX, Grant MacEwan College, Coca Cola, Sun Life, Scotia Bank,

CFCW Radio, AMA Travel, Budget Rent a Car and Direct Cremation

The bride and groom were happy but could have been happier if the best man had not been involved in a fist fight in the parking lot with Charity's brother and the caterer had not forgotten to deliver the bottled Coke and Sprite. Ed was almost in a screaming mood as 150 guests wanted to put a little mix with their liquor

Another reason Ed was tearing his hair out was because the guest book suddenly disappeared and someone prematurely released twelve pigeons outside the community hall and no fireworks were available for that night. Also the band, Rock Tunes Five, was late in arriving because the musicians couldn't find the hall.
And then when the instruments were in place the master of ceremonies asked the band leader that the tunes; *Roll Me Over In The Clover*, *Hokey Pokey*, *Goodnight Moon*, *Good Night Stars*, *Good Night Broken-down Cars*, *We're All Conservatives, and The Bank Foreclosed My Home*, not be played.

When the Coke and Sprite arrived, the bar opened for the night and the reception began with the groom and bride receiving good wishes and hand shakes from those invited who were mostly realtors from the Best Realty where Ed worked, and the neighbors and friend of the Cane and Remus families.

The reception progressed smoothly with Reverend Wendy Bush from Lac La Biche saying grace. Most of the focus during the meal was on Alberta grown pot roast beef and British Columbia champagne until a bone got stuck in the bride's throat. A guest of the two families, Dr. Hardy, removed the bone without much of a commotion.

This was followed by burst of laughter and cheers as the guests banged their cutlery against their plates suggesting that the bride and groom should stand up and kiss,
And when they did, each time it wasn't just a peck on the cheek but a veritable tongue-lashing. In between each stand/kiss/sit the master of ceremonies read congratulatory telegrams.

Among a list of telegrams one was from Chief Mike Boyle of the Edmonton Police Service that read: "Ed, I'm sorry you had trouble with your tire. Just a reminder that your guests at the reception remain sober"

Another read: "As soon as your honeymoon is over, just a reminder that you can get a good deal on your furniture. Nothing down, no interest and two years to pay. Congratulations Charity and Ed. – the Brick"

Another congratulatory message read: Ed and Charity, congratulations on reaching an important step in your life. Remember however, both of you have neglected to file you last income tax return. Signed – Revenue Canada.

Another congratulatory telegram read: "Sorry I'm unable to attend your wedding reception. At this moment I'm campaigning for a possible October election - Gosh the war in Afghanistan, Global Warming and the high price for gasoline have become major issues."
Prime Minister Stephen Harper.

Although invited to the wedding opposition leader Stephane Dion decided to stay in Ottawa. His telegram read: "Sorry that I'm unable to attend your wedding. As you know I'm in charge of a minority Liberal opposition. I'm preparing for the next Conservative budget and forming coalition with the NDP and Block parties. To say the least it's stormy in Ottawa. Hope you have a little son.

Congratulations Charity and Ed

Then it was the MC's turn to propose a champagne toast to the bride and groom but when he pried the bottle cork open it flew upward bouncing off the ceiling and ending on one of the bridesmaid's bowl of soup. He then he continued, "I now propose a toast to the bride's throat. Don't you think Dr. Hardy did an excellent job in removing a bone from it?"

Some laughed, some smiled, while others booed believing meat getting stuck in one's throat was a reflection on Alberta beef.

The MC apologized and then quoted Montaign, an essayist who lived in the 14th century and at one time said, 'Marriage is like a bird cage: It seems that birds outside are desperate to get in and those inside desperate to get out'.

At any rate may both of you have a long and happy life. And please remember eighty percent of married men cheat on their wives in Canada."

"How about the remaining twenty percent?" one of the guests hollered.

"The rest cheat while holidaying in Hawaii, Mexico, Florida or Thailand."

Those present laughed uproariously."

As soon as the MC toasted the bride and groom the best man proposed one whose punch line was, "Marriage is an institution but who wants to live in one," and then Charity's father who discarded has farm clothing and was dressed his Sunday best, took over and then said, "My experience is that a successful man is one who makes more money than his wife can spend, but a successful woman is one who can find such a man. I think Charity did."

This done, Ed's father, who was an oil company executive, took over and his punch line was, "Like in the oil industry love is a matter of chemistry. Charity, make sure Ed doesn't treat you like toxic waste."

Then Ed as the groom stood up and in his poetic toast said:

"Charity, here's a toast to you and me,

In our lifetime I hope we never disagree,

But if, perchance, we ever do,

Then here's to me and, and the heck with you."

The guests burst out with laughter and when the laughter died down Ed continued:

"Charity, I did not mean that, what I meant was may our married life be long and happy,

The cares and sorrows few;

And the friends around us remain faithful and true.

I now propose a toast to my beautiful wife, my bride and joy."

By the time toasting concluded and the photographer, a practical joker, had taken pictures of the wedding party, and then unknown to Charity and Ed he secretly collected keys from members of the guests.

Then when the MC spoke again he said, "Ladies and gentlemen, Charity realizes that that Ed has had a lot of girl friends before she became his bride.

"I understand that there were: Alfa, Eugenia, Lisa, Trisha and many more until he met Charity. Well, Charity at this time would greatly appreciate if any of them are here tonight and have keys to his condo returned."

On a cue from the photographer for all female key participants to bring their keys forward to the head table, ten women showed up, five disguised being pregnant and two as grandmas. One used a cane and the other a walker.

Guests and friends oh, how they laughed at that moment and when the laughter died down each person went to the bar to have another drink.

Charity then enlivened the party a bit more by believing Ed had the finest voice in Edmonton and exclaimed, "Ed, do sing us something!"

Ed got up, smiled and turning to his bride tried to think of something suitable for the occasion, something with seriousness from the past and began to sing, *"The Old Gray Mare Ain't What She Use to Be."*

The band drum banged, the fiddle growled, the saxophone blared and then Charity herself and the guests joined in singing the chorus.

The loud blend of voices and music, like a hurricane, shook the hall inside, and outside in the parking lot it seemed as if there was an alarm and under a silver half-moon and shining stars in the sky nocturnal creatures: owls, bats, night hawks, coyotes, skunks and even birds that have no wings but can fly at night participated in the celebration., Even frogs in the nearby pond croaked wishing Charity and Ed happiness every minute of their life.

The celebration began when all the animals and birds in the Edmonton Zoo signed a promissory note that neither animal nor bird would be harmed. Then the monkeys sent out invitation cards with kind regards and suggested the guests be dressed in their fashion best. With this in mind Elsie the Elephant who acted as master of ceremonies said to each animal and bird to be at ease but a poodle named Doodle said, "I'm unable to be at ease because I'm always chasing fleas."

A duck said, "Our forests are being destroyed by oil tycoons and many of my friends die after getting stuck in tailing ponds and therefore the invitation should have been made void"

A Canada goose agreed and said, "We should protect our birds and animals as they are without a measure a Canadian treasure."

Hearing the news a parrot began to swear.

"Oh, dear. Don't cuss," cried out an octopus.

A baboon emailed a message that he couldn't attend because he had an appointment to ride in a hot air balloon.

A crab came to the reception in a cab and played *Never Say Goodbye* with a fork and a spoon while on his horn a unicorn played the tune *You Are My Everything*.

At this point in time Elsie said, "Attention please. All the guests are now ready to dine, dance and cheer. At the bar we have Coke and Sprite but no beer."

"I fear I can't hear what Else had to say," said a deer.

A beaver after having several sips of his drink explained to the deer what Elsie had said and then sang a song about a chimpanzee that had a sore knee. The song was *A Groovy Kind of Love.*

A dolphin then sang *Everybody Should Love Someone Sometime* and another about seeing a school of mermaids in West Edmonton Mall.

Next the king of the beasts, the lion, said to Elsie" Excuse me while I have another Coke."

"Leo must have had a glass of wine instead of a Coke," said the porcupine and with a shout to the trout said, "Did you notice how Leo smacked his lips?"

"I'd smack mine too," said a Kangaroo If I wasn't sitting next to you."

A short time later Elsie bowed reverently and said, "Listen dear animals and birds to what I have to say.

The king of the animal world must have his way and now it's time to eat and dance. First on the menu the birds prepared a delicious bird's nest soup and then we can enjoy other stuff including a dish of Moose Lake fish."

A caribou then presented a toast to Ed and Charity. As soon as this was done and tables cleared Elsie said, "Listen everyone, let's rejoice, sing and dance."

To which a whale replied. "I can't dance because I lost my tail," and a raccoon picked up a broom and said, "I'm so happy I could dance all night."

A peacock and a grizzly bear put on their dancing shoes and were a on a tear as they danced the vibrant cha cha.

When completed Elsie urged other animals and birds not to stand around and gossip but to pair-up and dance some more. You may not believe this but a gopher paired up with a squirrel. a quail with a snail, a turtle with a weasel, a dog with a cat, Everyone in the parking lot, began dancing, leaping scurrying flying and stumbling.

There were no arguments or fights until an ass named Jack accidently kicked a badger in the rear end. That's when a magpie flew onto a table and still able, alleged the kick was done intentionally. Jack denied the allegation and to the magpie replied. "Kiss my ass." and made his exit.

Despite the small commotion there was a lot of emotion until midnight, when Elsie blew her trunk which woke up a dozing skunk and after yawning said, "I have just been handed a note from a goat and a sheep that its midnight and since everyone is exhausted so it's time to go home and sleep."

Meanwhile back inside while Charity and Ed were singing Ed blew his nose with the sound of a trombone and amid the general emotion and commotion, not to be outdone Charity's brother turned the reception topsy-turvy when he tried to show the bride and groom that he could dance. He leaped on one of the tables snapping his fingers above his head and did strange fancy steps which aroused Charity's father who was slightly intoxicated by now, swore at him but Charity's brother continued dancing. Charity's father then cried out in a voice like thunder, "Hey! We are tired of your acrobatic tricks!" and tried to expostulate him.

Penny's brother was finally ejected from the hall but not before he had another black eye. But then Rosa, the maid of honor, jumped onto the same table and sang songs which were rather risqué.

Rosa was a little role of fat with very short legs and active as a squirrel. Between each verse she stopped singing in order to have a mouthful of nuts which were in the centerpiece at the head table. But then when she did several wheel carts, she too was taken away.

While punctuated with music and laughter Charity and Ed next opened their presents and among a variety of gifts

were a television set, microwave oven, a handyman tool
set, enough linen and towels to last a lifetime, a potato
peeler, a play football, a yo-yo and a rolling pin.

A half-hour later Charity and Ed planted themselves in
front of a wall.
Charity then turned her back to a group of unmarried
women and flung her bouquet towards them.
Unfortunately the trajectory of the bouquet was such that
it landed on top a chandelier and there were no ladders
available to retrieve it so instead those present chanted,
"Throw your bra, throw your bra…"
Next from under Charity's dress Ed pulled out a garter.
He turned his back towards a group of marriageable men
and flung it towards them.
There was a scramble to retrieve the garter but unfortunately
Ed's best man, got trampled in the rush and resuscitation
had to be given. By the time he recovered the wedding
cake collapsed from the weight of the candles and there
were no pieces available for the guests to taste.
As soon as the tables were cleared the party went on until
1:30 a. m. with rockin' and rollin', two-stepping and fox-
trotting and waltzing. Ed and Charity danced the *Minute
Waltz* in thirty seconds.
Why only 30 seconds? Because Penny's right shoe heel
came off and the maid of honor forgot to include *Krazy
Glue* in the bride's emergency tote bag that included just-
in-case items: pain reliever, smelling salts extra panty
hose and tampons.
The ceremony officially came to a close when Ed and
Charity finally took to the floor and the band played, "The
Last Dance."

As soon as the reception ended and the band had left Ed and Charity realized their parents hadn't made arrangements to clean the hall, which had to be cleaned because Sunday school classes were scheduled later in the morning.

By he time Ed and Charity arrived at their bridal suite it was 4:00 a.m. And when they entered they couldn't believe their eyes – windows were left open and suite was filled with mosquitoes.

Ed and Charity couldn't find anyone in management to rectify the problem nor could they get another room so they crawled into bed and covered themselves with a feathered quilt and slept until noon.

For those planning to get married Ed and Charity have two pieces of advice. First about marriage – don't get angry when you are faced with sleeping under a feathered quilt as a feather may get stuck in your ear. The second advice is about the wedding itself. When it comes to planning one, don't rely on relatives. Maybe you can arrange to have your reception at McDonald's. After all you get an Alberta beef Big Mac and all those party hats. Ed and Charity had no difficulty in adjusting to their new life.

THE BANFF HONEYMOON

CHAPTER 10

Hawaii has everything. Sand for the children, sun for the family, and sharks for the mother- in-law.

Its surprising the obstacles Ed and Charity had to overcome in order to enjoy their honeymoon not in Hawaii but in Banff, Alberta. In order to reach Banff from Edmonton they had to drive south up and down along the Queen Elizabeth Highway 2 and then west from the east where the Trans Canada Highway takes over at Calgary. This part is a great stretch of land made up of foothill mountains, lakes and forests where, moose, deer, elk and bear run free.

With a "Just Married" sign hanging from the rear bumper of his Buick Regal Ed was first cruising along Queen Elizabeth Highway 2 and got frustrated by the slow traffic in front of him so pushed the pedal to the floor dodging in and out among slower vehicles which included large transport trucks. Ed seemed convinced that the one-way two-lane highway actually had three lanes with an imaginary third lane in the middle for passing, both directions at the same time in a hair-raising game of chicken.

Next, surprising, the result of dangerous mix of low and high speed traffic Ed was stopped by a cop for running a red light in Red Deer. The cop asked Ed for his driver's license and after seeing it said, "It looks like a genuine license but tell me because the way you drive how in the world did you get it?" and handed Ed a ticket.

As Ed was leaving Red Deer he noticed a billboard warning motorists to drive safely. The sign in large bold letters read: *Drive Safely. Keep Your Eyes Open On The Road.* Ed had his eyes open on a dead gopher in front of him when he was rear-ended by another motorist who was reading the same sign. Ed's bumper was ruined only slightly so both motorists continued on their way without exchanging names and addresses.

Near Airdrie Ed was stopped again, for speeding this time. As most people do, Ed wanted to argue with the cop about how fast he was going.

"I'm certain I wasn't going 140 kilometers in a 110 zone," Ed said while irritated. "How do you now my speed? I didn't see radar any place."

"We didn't catch you with a radar trap," this cop replied. "We spotted and timed you by helicopter patrol."

At the Junction where Highway #2 and the Trans Canada converge Ed and Charity stopped at a Truck Stop for lunch and each ordered a hamburger, French fries, cheesecake and a cup of coffee.

Just as the food was placed in front of Ed and Charity three rough-looking, long-haired, tattooed motorcycle drivers pulled off their helmets and seeing Ed's car ripped off the **Just Married** sign.

Then they went inside, harassed the bride and groom with derogatory remarks, grabbed their food and divided it among themselves.

Ed and Charity did not say a word. They got up quietly, paid their bill and continued their journey towards Banff. After they had driven away, a member of the motorcycle gang said to the owner of the truck stop, "He sure wasn't much of a man, was he?"

"I guess not," the truck stop operator replied, "And not much of a driver either."

"What do you mean?"

"He just ran over three motorcycles as he backed his car out of the parking lot."

Seeing the damaged motorcycles a second gang member became angry and said, "Mark our word, we'll get even with him soon."

In Calgary a patrolman stopped Ed for the third time. Ed didn't think he was speeding so he asked the patrolman, "What's wrong?"

"You are driving without a rear signal light, sir."

Ed got out of the car and opened the trunk. Suddenly he went to pieces. "Oh, oh!" he cried out. "How in the world could this happen?"

"Calm down," the officer said. "Driving without a rear signal light isn't that serious of an offence."

"Rear signal light? I don't care about the signal light. What about our luggage? We forgot in Edmonton."

After Ed was given another violation ticket he became tired after driving all the way from Edmonton and tried to register at several motels only to find all rooms had been taken because it was the height of the tourist season. Ed and Charity were having the same experience at the Holiday Inn.

"I'm sorry," the night clerk apologized. We don't have a room left in this place. Every room has been booked in advance. I'm terribly sorry, sir, that we can not accommodate you."

Knowing something about the service industry Ed said, "I know for example, that you always hold back a room or two for emergencies. Do you mean to tell me that if the Prime Minister Stephen Harper came here tonight you wouldn't find a room for him?"

"I guess you are right," the night clerk apologized. "We strain a point and would find something for the Prime Minister."

"Fine, then give us the room because I know the Prime Minister Harper won't be here tonight. I have first hand information that he is in Ottawa getting ready for the next election"

The night clerk gave Ed and Charity the room and after they registered and were alone, Ed picked up Charity and carried her through the threshold at the same time saying, "At last my darling."

"At last what?"

"At last we are really one."

"Yes, dear," Charity said. "But from the practical point of view it would be advisable to order dinner for two."

Ed got on the phone and ordered a bucket of Kentucky fried chicken that was delivered to their room.

During the night when it was time to go to sleep Charity got tired of standing, wandered into the bedroom and crawled into bed. Ed meanwhile stood by a window gazing at the flowing Bow River, full moon, sparkling stars and northern lights that almost could be heard, racing back and forth in the sky.

"Dear," Charity called, "Why don't you come to sleep?"
"Because."
"Because, what?"
"Because my mother told me that if I ever got married this would be the most wonderful night of the year and I'm not going to miss it. The Rocky Mountains in the distance are beautiful."

Charity had gone over the honeymoon scene a hundred times in her mind. Ed would carry her over the threshold and murmur sweat endearments. His lips would find hers and they would move to the bedroom. It is true that when Ed and Charity registered he carried Charity over the threshold but after watching the river, moon and stars the love-making for Charity was finished before it began. Ed had fallen asleep and Charity lay in bed wondering if she ever would become pregnant.

Late in the morning Ed and Charity entered the Holiday Inn Restaurant for breakfast and sat on a stool. At the counter, to be helpful, the waitress while handing each a menu, said, "I have spare ribs, hog liver, chicken legs and…"
"Hold it," Ed interrupted the waitress. "You have your troubles and we got ours. Why don't you skip your sad story and order each of us bacon and eggs, toast and a cup of coffee?"
As soon as the waitress placed the order she returned to the spot where Ed and Charity were sitting and said, "You say you got troubles? What kind of troubles?"
"We do have a problem," Ed admitted. "My wife wants a German shepherd dog for security sake but the price I can get one for is $1,000. That's too much."

"I'll say it is. You are getting ripped off. I can get you one for $200."

"Am I ever gland we ran into you? How soon can you deliver the dog?" Charity asked.

"Let me make a phone call and I'll let you know," the waitress replied and went to a phone to make her call.

The dog was delivered within an hour. What the waitress did was to phone SPCA but that did not matter, what did, Charity felt she would be protected at a time Ed was away selling real estate. "Thank you, thank you," Charity said as Ed paid for the dog and placed the animal in the back seat of the car.

Ed and Charity were on the Trans Canada Highway again heading towards Banff when they decided to stop at Canmore to admire the scenery and find out why it was the fastest growing community in Canada. As soon as Ed opened the car door the dog jumped out and took after a cat. In spite of much whistling, calling, horn blowing and waiting for several hours the dog did not return so the new bride and groom decided to place an ad in the Canmore newspaper.

"You are late for today's edition," the editor said as soon as Ed and Charity walked into the newspaper office. "This issue of the paper goes to press in another fifteen minutes."

"I wish you could squeeze the ad some place," Charity pleaded. "This is a valuable dog and we are offering a $200 reward."

"Write the ad up," the editor said. "If it's that important we'll hold the presses another fifteen minutes." Charity wrote the ad, paid for it and with Ed headed back to their car. Ed was about to start the engine when it occurred to

Charity that she had not included the phone number in the ad and both rushed to the newspaper office expecting everyone being busy. Instead there was no one around except the janitor. The presses weren't running and no one was in the office.

"Where's everybody?" Charity asked the janitor." I expected to see presses running and everybody working."

"Oh!" the janitor said. "They stopped the presses and everybody took off five minutes ago. They are looking for someone's dog which if found, there's a $200 reward."

Ed and Charity never did find the dog and at the outskirts of Banff spotted a billboard that read: Cowboy Bill's Auto Service. *Try Us Once and You'll Never Go Anywhere Else.*

Here the Trans Canada Highway was in such deplorable shape that Ed drove into a deep pothole which was filled with mud and water that splashed the car engine, killing it dead.

It cost $50 to have the car towed to Cowboy Bill's Service and another $100 to get the engine repaired.

When Ed and Charity were ready to take off Charity said to Cowboy Bill, who repaired the engine, "Why don't you fill the hole with dirt?"

Cowboy Bill's answer was, "It's hard to do during daytime because of the heavy traffic. You must remember that over 30,000 vehicles pass through Banff each day."

Charity then asked, "Then why don't you fill it during night time?"

Cowboy Bill was candid, "I confess that business is slow these days and that's when I fill the hole with water."

As soon as Ed and Charity reached the town of Banff they registered at the Fairmont Springs Hotel and did what other tourists do in the National Park: escape being gored by an elk or attacked by a grizzly bear. The also bathed in the Sulpher Springs Swimming Pool, visited the Museum, rode the tramway to the top of Sulpher Mountain and shopped at souvenir shops for something to bring home

At one of the shops Ed purchased a beautiful peace pipe with an intricate Indian design, which included strange writing. Ed thought he would give the pipe to Charity, now that the dog was lost, so he asked the clerk to translate the writing.

"Very easy," the clerk said, "It says smoking may be hazardous to your health."

Charity meanwhile purchased a slingshot with the words *I Visited Banff* inscribed on the handle. This was no ordinary slingshot made out of cheep plastic from China but one made of Canadian metal. Instead of using stone pebbles this slingshot could use golf balls, which when fired, could travel 100 yards at speeds of up to 100 feet per second.

Charity also purchased a blue budgie bird in a cage just in case Ed was out of town she had someone to talk too.

Next Ed and Charity were driving on a one-way street and met up with a moose that refused to leave their route. His antlers wee huge, really huge. It seemed that a laser beam from a galaxy controlled this wild animal.

The faster Ed went so would the moose kicking up gravel. Suddenly a stone the size of a golf ball struck the windshield cracking it from top to bottom.

Can you imagine how alarmed Charity became? It's difficult to believe that Ed would not harm this moose right then and there but he didn't because he kept his pledge that by being a member of the Moose Lodge he was not to harm a moose in any way.

The moose eventually disappeared but not before Ed met a park policeman screaming, "Hey, there! Where do you thing you're going?"

"To the Banff Springs Hotel but I must be late because all the cars are coming back."

As the policeman approached closer he asked, "Didn't you see the arrows?"

"Arrows?"

Then the cop asked, "Do you know why I pulled you over?"

Charity, uptight without thinking, replied, "Because my husband couldn't catch the other cars."

"No," the cop said, "Why I pulled you over is because you are on a one-way street."

"But I was going one way," Ed said.

It was here that Charity interrupted the conversation and while pointing a finger at Ed said rather sarcastically, "See, didn't I tell you not to follow the moose, and besides that you drove on the wrong side of the lane and didn't turn on your signal lights. Now what have you got to say?"

"The patrolman turned towards Ed and asked, "Who is that woman with you?"

"That's my bride, Charity. We are on our honeymoon."

"Well, sir, drive on," the patrolman said, "Looks like you are in enough trouble without me giving you a ticket. Enjoy your stay in Banff."

But things weren't enjoyable the following day when Ed like a foolish tourist invaded the backyard of grizzly bear territory near a public picnic site. Ed expected the bear to

be tame and was shocked when he was taking a snapshot
of the animal it attacked him. Since there was no use
arguing with a bear and there is no such a thing as bear
politics or plea bargaining, Ed was cornered and had no
option but to fall to his knees and pray. Ed was surprised
however, when the bear suddenly stopped attacking him
and got on his knees also.

"That's marvelous," Ed said to the bear, "You joining me
in prayer when I was giving up myself for being dead."

The bear made loud, grunting noises which translated
from bear language into English meant, "Don't interrupt
sir, as I'm saying grace before I have you for my meal."

Seeing the difficulty Ed was in Charity picked up the
slingshot she had purchased, inserted a golf ball and with
all her strength stretched the elastic and let it go – zing!
Within a split second the golf ball struck the hungry bear
on the head stunning it momentarily.

As soon as the bear scampered into the wilderness
and Ed recovered from the shock of being attacked, he
and Charity returned to the hotel where the following
afternoon they decided to play a round of golf. Their game
was progressing nicely until the 16th hole when Charity's
ball landed in the middle of an elk herd and four bulls.

With a giant rack on each head, the bulls began fighting
among themselves right on top of the ball. Both Charity
and Ed were afraid to approach the fighting elk fearing
if they got near one; the animal would gore them in the
rear end.

"So why don't you charge the bulls away with a golf cart?"
Charity suggested and that's what Ed did but not before
the elk with the largest rack tipped over the cart and struck
Ed on his rear sending him five feet into the air.

Prior to that Ed managed to go out of bounds on the 15th hole while Charity went out of the bounds on the 16th and they went into the 17th hole tied. The hole was a long par 3 – 195 yards. It seemed even longer on a hot summer day. Ed had the honor to teeing-off first using a 5 iron and came within several feet of the pin. Charity planted her ball in the middle of a pond nearly hitting a Canada goose. What was good for the goose wasn't for Charity and that did it.

After going through the motion of playing out the 18th holed Ed and Charity parked their carts at the clubhouse and returned to the hotel where in the lobby they ran into Ed's friend from Calgary, Sammy Helper, who was registered in the same hotel after getting married on the same day in Calgary that Ed and Charity did.

While Sammy and Ed were alone Sammy whispered to Ed, "Ed, boy, let's see who can perform our manly duties the most often tonight. I'll wager you a case of Labatt's Kokanee beer that I can do it more often with my bride Lisa, than you can with Charity."

Ed agreed to the challenge and that night he and Charity made love 2 different times, each time marking a stroke (1) on the bedroom wall.

The following morning Sammy entered Ed's and Charity's room and asked, "Well, how many times did you and Charity do it?"

Ed pointed to the 2 strokes on the wall (11), which surprised Sammy.

"Wow!" he cried out, "You surprise me. You did it eleven times. Do you want to know something?"

"What?"

"You beat Lisa and me by 4 times."

The following morning when Charity rolled out of bed she excitedly asked Ed, "Where is our car dear?"

"I parked it and the hotel parking lot last night."

"But it's not there."

"It has to be there," Ed said as he jumped out of the bed and then mentally retraced the evening when he last saw the car. "We went to the Sulpher Springs pool spa and stayed there until it closed at midnight."

"Finally it registered, "Someone must have stolen my antique pink colored Mercedes."

"Cars don't get stolen in Banff. This is a honeymoon town like Niagara Falls and not like Edmonton where there's a stabbing each night and teenagers cruise the alleys and rip off wheels for excitement."

"But it's gone. Now what do I do?"

"Call the police," Charity suggested.

Instead of phoning Ed took Charity by the arm and walked to the RCMP office.

As soon as they explained what had happened the constable on duty said, "I know how you feel. That's what I went through when my car was stolen."

"A police car stolen?" Charity said.

"That's right. Car theft these days are so routine in every city that even policemen who take theft reports have their vehicle stolen."

The officer then had Ed fill out a car-theft report in which he wrote," I parked my car at midnight and it wasn't there when Charity and I woke up this morning."

Glancing at the report the officer asked, "Was the tank full?"

"Three quarters."

"Then they could be driving around for a while."

Ed didn't get a sense of urgency that a crime-fighting approach was mobilized on his behalf and then was given a file number for the insurance company.

As Ed and Charity were making their exit the Mountie said, "If the car is found police will get in touch with you."

Ed and Charity returned to their hotel room where Ed phoned his insurance agent in Edmonton who said, "Because this involves theft of an entire vehicle, I'll hear from the insurance company and then phone you in Banff."

"You mean to say there's theft of parts of vehicles?" Charity asked.

"There is. I see where there's a lot you have to learn about car insurance."

That afternoon Ed called the police station asked the dispatcher if his Buick Regal had been located. The dispatcher punched the license number into a computer and announced, "Still outstanding, sir."

Ed and Charity decided it was a waste of time sitting around and waiting for the phone to ring so they walked the streets and alleys of Banff to see if thieves had ditched the car.

They hadn't. In the evening Ed again checked with the police but the officer on duty said, "Still outstanding, sir."

Ed felt totally devastated until the insurance agent in Edmonton phoned and said, "Ed, the loss-of use clause in your policy pays for the use of a rental car."

And then the agent explained that if the car wasn't recovered in a week it probably would never be recovered.

The agent also said that the insurance company would wait about a month before settling the claim. "Call if you hear anything."

In order to expedite the car recovery Charity suggested placing an ad in the Banff newspaper and offering a reward.

"An excellent suggestion but I'll first check with the police," Ed said and when he and Charity did check, the officer on duty said, "First the very process of offering a reward for a stolen car will create its own stolen market, criminals stealing cars to claim the reward. Plus police won't supervise the rewards."

The officer went on to say that there was nothing to prevent Ed from placing an ad in a newspaper, television or radio but gave several things to consider.

"If joy riders have taken the car and wrapped it around a pole or a tree we would already known about it. If people are to recognize the car in a parking lot, you'll have to provide some identifying feature aside from the pink color. In your case, is there such a feature?"

"Other then the horn going 'toot, toot', it plays a musical tune and then there's the license plate."

"Forget the license plate. It won't be on the car."

Next the officer explained that if Ed wanted to offer a reward he would have to deal with sleazebags who would phone and say something like, 'Give me $500 and I'll tell you where your car is,' And once you get this supposed lead you'll have to check it out yourself because police don't have he time going around after all the losers this type of an ad may attract."

By now Ed was convinced that his Buick Regal would not be found until the following morning when police phoned and an officer on the other end said, "Sir, we have located your burgundy colored Buick."

The first question Charity asked was, "What shape is it in?"

"Some parts are missing and there's damage to the ignition. You'll also need a new paint job. Otherwise it doesn't appear severe."

"Any idea who may have stolen the car?"

"We are not dealing with kids or joy riders. The thieves are professionals from Calgary."

"How did you reach that conclusion? Was it through finger prints?"

"And a tip from Calgary police. It appears that three riders had their motorcycles run over at a truck stop. Each biker filed a damage report which had a signature. The signatures and finger prints on your vehicle which was dumped, matched."

"Dumped? Where?"

"It was found on an isolated road near the Columbia Ice field."

Ed immediately phoned the insurance agent in Edmonton who made arrangements to have the car towed to Cowboy Bill's Auto Service to have it repaired and painted. And Cowboy Bill said, "Your car will be ready tomorrow evening."

When 'tomorrow evening' arrived Ed went to have the car picked up but unfortunately Cowboy Bill said, "We are still waiting for parts from Calgary."

It was on the final day of Ed's and Charity's honeymoon that the missing parts were replaced and a new paint job given. The problem however, was that Ed's 1993

Buick Regal was an old model and paint manufacturers discontinued making the color burgundy. Cowboy Bill risked his life and painted a bright yellow instead. But this did not matter as far as Ed was concerned. What did was that he had his car back; the Banff honeymoon was over and as soon as they returned to Edmonton Charity would do his laundry, iron his clothing and cook meals for him.

And as his parents predicted, Ed's real estate sales increased tremendously because by now homes that normally sold for $150.000, because of the oil boom in Alberta, sold for $400,000.

CHAPTER 11

As soon as Ed and Charity returned to Edmonton they discovered the condo ceiling had sprung a major leak and there weren't enough catch basins in the city to prevent water from flooding the living room and the carpet, which had to be replaced. As soon as Ed finished replacing the carpet he noticed a lump under in the middle of the floor. Ed felt his shirt pocket for his cigarettes but found they were missing. Ed wasn't about to tear up the carpet so he stood on the lump jumping up and down until the lump disappeared and the new carpet was smooth. Satisfied that there was no lump Ed gathered his tools and carried them to the car. As Ed opened the door two things happened simultaneously. Ed found his cigarettes on the front seat and on his shoulder Charity's hand as she said, "Ed have you seen my budgie bird which I bought while on our honeymoon?"

"I haven't and do want to know something else?"

"What?"

"I don't like your budgie bird."

That night Ed and Charity had a domestic dispute over the missing blue-coloured bird which had a mania for flying around the condo and scattering droppings everywhere. Several droppings had landed on Ed's head, which struck Charity funny. During a heated argument that followed

Charity quaking with fury. Screamed, "Ed, if you don't get me another budgie bird I'm going to call the police!"

"Unbelievable," Ed thought. "Married for one week and already she's taking control of my life. Who does Charity thing she is? I have married Miss Right but didn't realize her first name was Always."

Ed slammed the door behind him and while pointing his finger at Charity said, "Charity, I beg you get some therapy. Believe me, I did not kill you budgie bird."

Ed then drove to his office at Best Realty where he slept on a couch that night. In the meantime Charity called police and her mother who asked, "Charity. How was your honeymoon?"

"Oh, Mamma," Charity replied. "We had our car stolen but the honeymoon itself was wonderful. Banff is such a romantic place." And burst into tears.

"But Mama, as soon as we returned home Ed and I had an argument and Ed used the most horrible language, things lie I seldom heard before. I mean all those four-lettered words."

"Charity," her mother said. "Calm down, what could be so awful" What four-lettered words did he use?"

"Please don't make me tell you," Charity wept. "I'm so embarrassed they're just too awful."

"Darling, you must tell me what four-letter words were used?"

Still sobbing Charity said, "Oh, Mama the words are dust, wash, iron and cook."

In the morning at the Best Realty office, to Ed's surprise, he was arrested as a cop said, "Ed Remus you have the right to be silent but if you decide to say something you will be misquoted, then what you say will be used against you."

Ed was finger printed and charged with hunting for birds without a license.

Ed was carted off to the Remand Centre and placed in a holding cell where 20 or so guys were exchanging drugs. After spending a night Ed said to a guard, ""Sleeping on a concrete floor with one eye open isn't much fun. One of the guys even said to me that if I didn't buy some of his drugs he would spit on my grave."

Hearing about Ed's arrest his parents came rushing to the Police Headquarters but were told, "Sorry Mr. and Mrs. Remus but your son has been charged and must stand trial."

The defendant is presumed innocent until proven guilty beyond a reasonable doubt did not matter what did, was that Charity's budgie bird was missing and Ed was the prime suspect. It was an open and shut case. At the time of the investigation the living room window as open and the entrance door was shut.

The following day a kangaroo-type trial took place. There was no kangaroo present however but Judge Black did resemble a kangaroo except that he had no tail and couldn't hop because of a sprained leg.

The prosecuting attorney Paul 'Boomer' Cross was a short stubby lawyer who wore spectacles, kept picking his nose and often said, "Whatever" or "As Prime Minister Trudeau use to say."

On the stroke of 10:00 a.m. there was silence in the court room when the clerk glanced towards Ed and said, "Ed Remus do you swear that the testimony you are about to give this court is the truth and the whole truth so help you God."

"I do."

As the two attorneys began debating the case, Ed's defense lawyer Thomas Huff said to Cross, "You are a dirty shyster and before this case is over I'll show you for the crooked ape you are."

And Cross retorted, "And you sir are a cheat and a liar."

"Come, come." Judge Black, who was tall in stature with a mustache, broke in and said, "Let's proceed with the Ed Remus case now that you have identified each other."

An when the trial began and following a short testimony the judge said to Ed, "How old are you?"

"Twenty four."

"Are you qualified to give a urine sample?"

"Only if you are qualified to ask for one."

"And what kind of a flower are you wearing in your lapel?"

"It's a dandelion your honour."

Judge Black was allergic to pollen but not to smoke exhaust fumes from vehicles and industrial smokestacks, sneezed, "Atchooo!" pounded his gavel and said, "Thirty days. Case closed."

An appeal for a lighter sentence was denied on the grounds that Ed had earlier faxed an uncomplimentary lawyer joke to the prosecutor. The joke was. What is the difference between a dead sunk and a lawyer? The answer of course is. "Skid marks in front of the skunk."

In jail, when the Reverend Taylor arrived to visit Ed, the pastor suggested, "You should make up with Charity. I'm certain she will forgive you."

Ed then asked if there was a remote chance Ed could end up in Heaven if he should die in jail.

"If you pray you may but until your prayers are answered you may have to spend some time in purgatory."

Ed would do anything to be free and sleep with Charity in the same bed. He was about to go on a hunger-strike when a remarkable development took place. The jail guard flung the door wide open exclaiming, "Ed Remus there has been a terrible mistake. You are a freeman. The budgie bird has been found!"

'Where? Where?"

"In the parking lot. Unfortunately a cat had eaten it partly."

"So I'm free?

"You are."

Relieved Ed sank to his knees and kissed the floor of the holding cell and as he made his exit his eyes were dull, his hair was turning grey for a man his age, and even his face seemed to have taken a graying hue that blended with the drab jail uniform he had worn.

"Although I'm free I feel as I no longer will be on this planet," Ed said to the guard and after shaking hands Ed made his exit.

The first thing Ed did once he was released was to go to the Pet Shop and purchase another blue colored budgie bird and Charity was pleased. From that day onward they hugged and kissed, adjusted to being married and slept in the same bed. And the real estate market was booming but Pollsters indicated that it soon would be blundering.

Ed was married during the month of August. A year later on a September warm day he was at the Borden Park outdoor swimming pool taking part in a charity Belly

Flop contest with proceeds going to Meals on Wheels to renovate its kitchen

A large crowd, each person paying ten-dollars, gathered at the pool bleachers to embrace the sun and watch an event billed as *Edmonton's Battle of the Bulges.* Contestants drew numbers as to when to dive, flex their muscles and display their physique.

When a whistle was blown for Ed to make his dive he climbed to the diving board, pulled in his stomach, puffed out his chest and a smile spread across his face. Once on the diving board in a blue colored swim suit he jumped up and down several times and then dove into the water as those present watched.

At the conclusion of the dive the announcer on the pubic address system said, "Ladies and gentlemen. I have some good news and some that is bad. The good news is that the judges have awarded Mr. Remus's magnificent dive a perfect score."

There was a thunderous applause.

"And the bad news is that during the dive Ed apparently because couldn't swim well, had a heart attack."

The audience moaned and groaned.

Hearing the PA announcer Reverend Taylor rushed to the spot where Ed landed and with the help of a lifeguard dragged him out of the pool where he was resuscitated.

Seeing Ed in excruciating pain the Reverend leaned over Ed's shoulder and asked, "Ed, have you made peace with God?"

In a faint voice Ed replied, "I didn't know I had an argument with Him."

Then the Reverend continued, "Do you believe in the Father, Son and Holy Spirit?"

And these were the last words Ed had spoken on Planet
Earth, "I'm dieing and you are asking me riddles."

Minutes later Dr. Hardy, who was also one of the
contestants, pronounced Ed dead with a supplementary
announcement, "And that's too bad because Ed was
scheduled to receive an honorary doctorate degree from
the University of Alberta."

A day after Ed had died his wife Charity, got into an
argument with Ed's parents if her husband and their son
should be buried or cremated.

They also argued what hymns to sing, use an organ or a
flute, should the casket be open or closed, should a private
service be held or one open to the public at the newly
renovated Shaw Conference Centre.

In the end it was agreed that Ed would be buried and to
hold the funeral at the No Name Universal Reformed
Church. The casket would remain open. Among the hymns
to be sung were *Amazing Grace* and *How Great Thou Art*
accompanied by an organ. After the burial at a municipal
cemetery there would be a wake at the Westmount
Community Hall and lunch served. The obituary notice
in the *Sun* read: "Rather than flowers, the family suggests
donations be made to Meals on Wheels."

Edmonton bid farewell to Ed Remus in a simple service
remembering him as a realtor whose state was Edmonton,
Alberta.

Some arrived early to pay their respect. Sammy Helper
who knew Ed all his life flew in from Calgary and publicly
said, "I have lost a true friend."

Outside the church several passers-by's enquiring about
the service reacted with difference and one even said, "So
Ed is dead. Who cares? Let them make a potpourri from
his fingernails and hair."

It is true that when Ed was alive there were people who said nasty things about him but as soon ad he died, they praised him.

Reverend Taylor said, "Ed Remus was the kindest and most generous young man I have ever known. Heaven will not be the same with Ed there."

Shortly after 1:00 p. m. church bells rang and a motorcade delivered Charity, her and Ed's parents. They made their way in silence up a flight of stairs into to the church and then the front pews where Ed's body lay in front of them in an open casket. Mourners listened to tributes as the mood of the service swung back and forth between grief and laughter. They all had to pause to shed tears or regain their composure as Reverend Taylor urged everyone to celebrate the real estate salesman who put Edmonton on the map of Alberta and helped Meals on Wheels out of debt."

"Charity, Ed loved you very much, "Reverend Taylor said. "We all know that, so don't cry. Think of Ed up there in Heaven with Saint Peter, Saint Michael the archangel and Rabbi Libowitch, Ed's friend who died recently."

Reverend Taylor then read words from the Bible and there wasn't a dry eye in the entire church as he said, "Ed Remus, this isn't the final chapter of your life. May your soul enter a retirement centre in Victoria B. C. or Heaven and may you be reincarnated. Till then rest in peace."

But Ed had little peace in Heaven initially because when he arrived at the queue outside the Pearly Gates there as there was a long line-up and Ed hated line-ups even on Planet Earth. Saint Peter while screening people spoke to the first, second and third and then eventually asked another, "Where are you from?"

"America," the elderly man in the lineup answered while waving the American flag.

"And what have you do to deserve admission to Heaven?" Saint Peter continued.

"I have helped President George Bush attack Iraq in order to get rid of Saddam Hussein.

"And many innocent civilians died because of the bombing," Saint Peter said and the Pearl Gates remained closed.

Saint Peter then turned to the man in front of Ed and asked, "And where are you from?"

"Germany."

'And what have you done to deserve admission into Heaven?"

"I've been a lawyer all my life, sir, and taken part in many complex lawsuits."

"Saint Peter began to escort the lawyer inside the gates, when the lawyer began to protest that his untimely death had to be some sort of a mistake.

"I'm much too young to die. I'm only thirty-eight," he said.

Saint Peter agreed that 38 did seem a bit young to be entering the Pearly Gate and went to another room to check on the case.

When Saint Peter returned he said to the German attorney, "I'm afraid the mistake may be your own doing, my son. We have verified your age on the bases of the number of hours you billed your clients, and you are at least 78. You must go to Hell."

Ed didn't wait for the question when it was his turn to be interviewed so he turned to Saint Peter and said, "I'm from Edmonton, Canada. Do I have to go to Hell too?"

Saint Peter took off his glasses, shook his head and said, "Edmonton? That's where it gets very cold in winter and hot during summer."

"That's right, sir," Ed said.

"Well, you have already been there." and along with a clergyman from Argentina was told to go inside the Pearly Gates.

"Reverend, here the keys to one of the nicest suites in Heaven," Saint Peter said to the clergyman."

And to Ed, "And you Mr. Remus, here are the keys to Heaven's penthouse where angels drift about, play harps and sing. It's a very nice place."

This upset Reverend Garcia who said, "Saint Peter, I don't understand this. I dedicated my entire life preaching the word of God and….."

"Listen Father," Saint Peter interrupted. "Clergymen are a dime a dozen here but this is the first real estate salesman we have seen in a long, long time."

The following Sunday parishioners at the No Name Universal Church in Edmonton prayed to Saint Peter, the gate keeper, to have just a glimpse of Ed in Heaven. Their wish was granted but in their horror the following Sunday they saw on a huge screen Ed with a beautiful blond on his lap.

"Ed! Ed!" they cried out. "How come you behave this way in Heaven, when you didn't chase married women while in Edmonton?"

Ed replied, "Listen, you people below in Edmonton. The blond is not my reward. I'm her punishment."

A month after Ed entered the Pearly Gates he was presented with a Chevrolet car by Saint Peter. This allowed Ed to travel all over Heaven until one day he met Rabbi Libowitch driving a Cadillac with a chauffeur. This amazed Ed. "Discrimination!" Ed thought and registered a protest with Saint Peter.

"Why would I get just a Chevy and Rabbi Libowitch a new Cadillac? We are both from Canada."

Saint Peter leaned over Ed's shoulder and whispered in his ear, "Look. Rabbi Libowitch is related to the Boss."

While Ed and Saint Peter were engaged in a conversation a Texas oilman who was allowed into Heaven appeared and got on Saint Peter's nerves. It seems that no matter what part of Paradise the Texan was shown it failed to measure up to the state of Texas. Finally Saint Peer took the Texan to the edge of Heaven so he could look straight into Hell and said, "Have you anything like this in Texas?"

"No," the Texan replied, "But I know some boys in Huston who can put it out."

As soon as Saint Peter was through dealing with the Texan two politicians from Italy arrived at the Pearly Gates but Saint Peter, because the two gents were implicated with the Mafia, refused to let them inside and in a thunder-like voice said, "Scram!'

As he said those words an angel flew by and said to Saint Peter, "You can't do that. Please go get them back."

Saint Peter ran off and came back exhausted. "They're gone!"

"The two Italians?"

"No. The gates," Saint Peter replied.

After the gates were recovered and Ed had been in Heaven for six months, Saint Peter said to Ed and Rabbi Libowitch that the portion of Heaven they were living in was about to be renovated.

"Go to Planet Earth and enjoy yourself. When the renovations are completed an angel will call on you when to return."

"Fine," Rabbi Libowitch said. I didn't do much traveling before so I'll travel to Israel."

"And I'll return to Edmonton and pick up my honorary doctorate degree in economics from the University of Alberta and while there, use their library to write poetry," Ed said.

Understanding Ed's poems requires intimate knowledge of the real estate industry, which according to scholars in Heaven, Ed had very little. Here are several limericks he wrote. A quick glance at these verses may encourage one to become a poet. If it doesn't its understandable.

A realtor named Jane Moroso	I'm not certain about my next verse
Displayed her torso	As a method of which to converse
A crowd soon collected	But it's clear to me
But no one objected	From what I can see
Some even hollered, "More so!"	In Heaven that's how words are disbursed

There was a tenant named Claire	I'll get it in a minute or two
Who had a magnificent pair	I like doing things for you
That's what she thought	I'm at your beck and call

Until she got caught
In the landlords
underwear

But doggone it all
There are things I
sometime must do

Amorous Sue

There's a lady from
Moline

Had a date she knew

Who writes limericks that
are clean

The coroner found

It wasn't her aim

The couple had drowned

To continue this game

While paddling a canoe

It's getting a bit obscene

An old Scottish realtor
from Skye

A realtor in Saskatoon

Reckoned "Old realtors
don't die"

Never learned how to eat
with a spoon

Though without any doubt

He would fork up his soup

When their heartbeat runs
out

With a bending stoop

Their sales will face with
a sigh

Too bad – he died to soon

There was a realtor named
Fred

An Edmonton realtor
named Rex

Who said as he climbed
out of bed

Alberta beef he always
rejects

"There's no heaven, I'm
sure

He lives on herbs

But I hate to endure
The alternative if I wake
up dead"

His appetite curbs
And slimmer and trimmer
he gets

As a realtor I made many
mistakes
In life those are
sometimes the breaks
I got married and joined
the crowd
Which made my mother
proud
For the good sense that it
makes

There was a realtor named
Joe
Who lost his 'get up and
go'
Almost without thinking

He began heavy drinking

And found his sales
astonishingly slow

Occasionally when I'm
blue
With nothing in particular
to do
I stand on my head

At the foot of the bed
And then shove my nose
in my shoe

My dog, Little Joe, can
hardly see
One day I took him for a
walk with me
When I felt something
warm
I looked down with alarm
Little Joe thought my leg
was a tree

When things go wrong, as they sometime will
My search for a lasting mate was uphill
When my funds were getting low and debts high
I wanted to smile but had to cry
So I kept taking a headache pill

Marriage is difficult to figure out
From the beginning it was a bout
I however, was determined to fight when hardest hit
And my parents urged me not to quit
Otherwise it would be a rout

My search in finding Charity had its twists and turns
And as everyone sometimes learns
Not to give up though the pace may seem slow
But then I received another rejection blow
Leaving my heart with scars and burns

Often I was frustrated and nearly gave up
When I thought I had captured the victors' cup
Another rejection came down
As I imagined my love mate wearing a wedding gown
In my dream she was sweeter than a toy Pomeranian
pup

But at last my search came to an end on a moonlit starry
night
I found Charity who now is my Mrs. Right
I have learned to fight back when hardest hit
And when things are rough one must never quit
And go through emotions of anger, depression, rejection
and fright

Dear Liberals in Ottawa, stop your bluster
And your taunt: "Filibuster!"
Michael Ignatieff go through with your threat
And make Stephan Harper sweat
To see how much election support the Conservatives can
muster

I'm betting the Conservatives don't have the numbers
They're bluffing following numerous blunders
But majority rules
When politicians don't act life fools
Or become stumblers

A *Collection of Real Estate Limericks by Ed Remus* stands
a distinct possibility of becoming the highest selling poetry
book in the history of publishing. Thanks to the release
of a compact and DVD disc by the same name, where Ed
reads his own poetry while in Heaven, worldwide sales
of the book have jumped to multi-million copies with
translations from Albanian to Zulu.

But even the remarkable achievement of the book it still
has a long way to beat the *Bible's* record of an estimated
six billion sales or the second biggest seller *Quotations*
from the works of Mao Tse-Tung, dubbed T*he Little Red
Book*, with sales of 900 million and included Asian humor
such as:
(1)   Passionate kiss like spiders web, soon lead to
       undoing of fly
(2)   Man who run in front of a car get tired
(3)   Man who run behind car get exhausted
(4)   Man who fly plane upside down have crack up
(5)   Man with one chop stick go hungry
(6)   Man who scratches ass should not bite finger
       nails
(7)   It takes many nails to build a crib but one screw
       to fill it
(8)   Foolish man give wife a grand piano, wise man
       give wife an upright organ

(9) Man who fight with wife all day get no piece at night

(10) Wife who put husband in doghouse soon finds him in cathouse

"At any rate sales have picked up dramatically since the video," said a Saint Peter's Publishing publicist who added, "And the spin-off potential is incredible."

Real Estate Limericks by Ed Remus has already spawned a healthy cottage industry in Edmonton featuring sales of T-shirts with the words "I've Been to Heaven and Back" emblazoned on the front. Other spin-offs planned by Saint Peter's Publishing that includes the works of Ed Remus are:

1   A diet book featuring Ed's favorite low fat recipes
2   A DVD of Ed doing exercises
3   An exotic fragrance inspired by Ed
4   Bobble-neck toys with Ed's image
5   A five-minute chit-chat with Ed on the Internet
6   A book entitled, 'How to get inside the Pearly Gates with no money down.'
7   Ed becoming a pay-for-view Heavenly talk-show host
8   A CD with Ed doing Heavenly bird calls
9   An Ed Remus monthly magazine on how one can reach Heaven without first going to Purgatory, and,
10   A board game titled, "Heavenopoly "

Ed then having an honorary doctorate degree returned to Heaven

EPILOGUE

Ed spent one year in Heaven and while there again met Archangel Michael who said to him, "Ed, there's a major crises on Planet Earth. Alberta needs you. You shall be incarnated so you can help ease an economic problem, especially in Edmonton, where there are spiraling house foreclosures and the only 'deposits' made on new cars are those made by birds flying over them. And it has nothing to do with media allegations that the recession is caused because of the sun and the moon."

Ed who was always willing to help anyone with a problem received permission from God to return to the Planet Earth.

Ed then said, "I can't wait to return to Planet Earth, see Charity and follow up on the recession that is taking place and assess the impact it is having on the City Of Champions. Being in Heaven will inspire me and have an impact on the rest of my life.

In the mean time all the money I made while in Heaven I will donate to charity."

While readjusting to earth's gravity Ed was back in Edmonton as a crack real estate salesman and an economic consultant. After analyzing the serious credit crunch in Canada Ed came to the conclusion that:

(1) If we spend money at Wal-Mart, the money will go to China

(2) If we spend money on gasoline, it will go to the Arabs

(3) If we purchase a computer, the money will go to India

(4) If we purchase a good car, the money will go to Japan

(5) If we purchase vegetables and fruit, the money will go to Mexico

(6) If we purchase something else, the money will go to Taiwan

(7) If we purchase diamonds the money will go to Africa

(8) If we purchase a Schumatz Hagen the money will go to Germany

(9) If we purchase crystal the money will go to the Czech Republic

(10) If we need special surgery the money will go to the United States

None of this will help the Canadian economy. Ed then suggested that in order to survive the crunch corporations should merge.

For example: Hale Business Systems, Mary Kay Cosmetics. Fuller Brush and W. R. Grace should merge to become - Hale, Marry. Fuller Grace. 3M and Goodyear should merge and become MMMGood. Frdex should merge with UPS to become FedUp. Fairchild Electronics and Honeywell Computers to become Fairwell Honeychild.

The bigwigs running the financial market took notice of Ed who then did a door-to-door survey about the global

recession and posed the question: "In Your Opinion How Bad is the Canadian economy, really."
The response was the following:

(1)   Its so bad that African television stations are now showing "Sponsor a Canadian child," commercials

(2)   Its so bad that the highest-paying job in Edmonton is jury duty

(3)   Its so bad a polygamist was seen on Jasper Avenue with only one wife

(4)   Its so bad the Canadian government is helping GM and Chrysler with a stimulus package

(5)   Customers at Costco are now buying only one roll of toilet paper

(6)   MacDonald's is introducing the mini ¼ - burger

(7)   Its so bad Prime Minister Harper has decided to lay off 15 Liberal senators

(8)   Foreign contract workers who hoped to become Canadian citizens are sent back to their homeland

(9)   At NHL games some fans have turned in their season tickets and the Edmonton Oilers instead of Paul Lorieau singing the national anthem now play a taped recording

(10)   Its so bad that Practical nurses are replacing RN's

(11)   Alberta premier Ed Stelmack is about to fire himself

(12)   The Enoch Cree Resort and Casino has asked to be managed by Somali pirates

(13)   Its so bad that 7 out of 10 homes in the Riverbend subdivision are in foreclosure

(14) The Alberta economy is faltering due to the plunging energy prices

(15) Its so bad that chickens in Alberta have stopped laying eggs and KFC is experiencing difficulty filling menu orders

(16) The Federal government is handing out free money to renovate homes

(17) Bottled water has become more expensive than a litre of gasoline

(18) Don Cherry is now purchasing his wardrobe at a Salvation Army Thrift Shop

(19) The picture is now worth only 200 words

(20) Its so bad gophers in Alberta are migrating to Saskatchewan

(21) Every penny counts so men are avoiding haircuts and growing beards

(22) Its so bad that IKEA is now selling funeral caskets.

(23) There are many signs that read: "Will Work free for Food and Lodging"

(24) Parishioners in some churches are placing Canadian Tire money in the collection baskets

(25) Its so bad that because of the market turmoil 115 banks in American collapsed and another 300 about to collapse

While Ed continued selling real estate and help solve the global economic crises Charity, having experience in husbandry and a swineherd at the Olds Agricultural College, helps Alberta Health Care find a cure for swine flu and research why so many honey bees are dieing.